Chicken Mission

The Mystery of Stormy Island

Jennifer Gray lives in London and Scotland with her husband, four children and a friendly but enigmatic cat. Her other work includes the Atticus Claw series and the Guinea Pigs Online books, co-written with Amanda Swift. The first book in the Atticus series, *Atticus Claw Breaks the Law*, was shortlisted for the Waterstone's Children's Book Prize and won the 2014 Red House Children's Book Award – Younger Readers category.

BY THE SAME AUTHOR

Chicken Mission

The Mystery of Stormy Island

JENNIFER GRAY

FABER & FABER

First published in 2016
by Faber & Faber Limited
Bloomsbury House, 74–77 Great Russell Street,
London WC1B 3DA

Typeset by Crow Books
Printed in the UK by CPI Group (UK) Ltd, Croydon, CR0 4YY

A CIP record for this book
is available from the British Library

ISBN 978–0–571–29833–4

FSC
www.fsc.org
MIX
Paper from
responsible sources
FSC® C101712

2 4 6 8 10 9 7 5 3 1

To my readers

With special thanks to all those who came up with
spectacularly evil villains

Prologue

Far to the north, on a remote clifftop, stands Stormy Cliff Caravan Park. The caravan park has seen better days — days when humans were content to spend their holidays huddled behind windbreakers eating damp sandwiches and drinking from thermos flasks of lukewarm tea. Now the holidaymakers have gone and the caravans have fallen into disrepair. The only visitors to the place are occasional birdwatchers and walkers. No one lives there except for a flock of chickens, which are tended to twice a week by the park keeper.

The one thing that hasn't changed over the years, however, is the view. On a clear day you can see for miles along the rugged, empty coastline and imagine a time millions of years ago, before humans ever existed; a time as far back as when dinosaurs walked the earth. For this part of the country is known for its fossils: it is a place where dinosaurs once congregated

by the shore and where their remains have been preserved in layer upon layer of chalk and clay.

The best of the fossils are to be found on Stormy Island – a bleak, towering hunk of rock that lies a little way out to sea, cut off from the mainland except at low tide when a rough stone causeway connects it to the beach below Stormy Cliff.

Stormy Island is not an inviting place: it is surrounded by jagged rocks and riddled with deep, dark, dangerous caves. Its main visitors are gannets and gulls. Few humans venture there and most of its fossil treasures have remained undiscovered.

That is, until now . . .

One chilly summer's morning at daybreak – before the chickens of Stormy Cliff had begun to stir – an enormous bird sat tall and erect on the branch of a tree on the cliff edge. The bird had, in fact, been sitting there like a statue for most of the night, watching the tide come in and cover the causeway, occasionally twisting its head very slowly round to the left, then round to the right, before fixing its unblinking, bright orange eyes

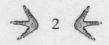

once again on the jagged outline of Stormy Island.

This bird did not need daylight to see the view. Nor did it need to shift its position to take in its surroundings. This bird was nocturnal, with binocular vision and a neck that could turn two hundred and seventy degrees in either direction. This bird was an eagle owl.

And it was here for a purpose.

Unsettled by the gathering light, the bird finally blinked. 'So, Vladimir,' it addressed itself in a series of clicks with its small, flat beak, 'you have found the perfect place at last. Now it is time to begin your experiments. But first, some breakfast.' The owl's sharp hearing caught the sound of the soft clucks and sighs of the chickens roosting in one of the nearby caravans. A pang of hunger almost undermined its resolve. It clicked its beak firmly. 'No, Vladimir,' it muttered, 'the chickens may be useful for your work. Besides, you do not want the humans to know you are here. They may try and return you to captivity.'

The owl looked about for something else to satisfy

its hunger. Its piercing eyes fell upon a rabbit nibbling a patch of grass a little way from the tree, oblivious to its presence. Measuring the distance with precision, the owl dropped noiselessly from its perch and grabbed the startled rabbit with its great, curved talons. Then with one flap of its wings it rose into the sky and, still clutching its limp prey, glided over the cliffs and across the sea towards Stormy Island.

Chapter One

'So, how fast can a chicken run?'

In the grounds of Dudley Manor at the Dudley Coop Academy for Chicks, Amy Cluckbucket was watching the month 4's science lesson. The lesson was being taught by Amy's brainy friend, Ruth. The two chickens were part of an elite-chicken squad whose job was to protect chickens everywhere from evil predators under the direction of their mentor, Professor Emeritus Rooster.

But today they were having a day off.

'Is it a) twenty-seven miles an hour, b) eighteen miles an hour, c) nine miles an hour or d) one mile an hour? Hands up for each one.' Ruth went through the choices again.

Amy scratched her head. She wasn't very good at running, or counting for that matter. She put her hand up for one mile an hour, which was about what she thought *she* could manage.

'And the answer is nine miles an hour!' Ruth said with a grin.

'Yay!' The chicks who had got the answer right congratulated each other with high fives. Amy felt slightly deflated. The chicks seemed to know a lot more than she did. She wished she'd paid more attention when she was at school.

Ruth raised her wings for calm. The chicks stopped talking immediately.

Amy was impressed. Ruth had an air of authority about her without being mean or shouting like some teachers did. Amy supposed it must partly be her appearance. Ruth was a tall white chicken with a long grey scarf and spectacles. It was the spectacles that gave her the edge, Amy decided.

'You've got to admit that nine miles an hour is pretty good,' Ruth said. 'Especially if you think that the fastest human runs at twenty-seven miles an hour, and he's about ten times taller than we are!' She put a slide on the screen showing the size of the human world-record holder compared to a chicken.

The chicks giggled. They were having a wonderful

time and learning lots in the process. Amy smiled at Ruth proudly.

'So, if chickens were ten times bigger, how fast would they run?' asked Ruth.

One of the chicks stuck its hand up. 'Ninety miles an hour?'

'Very good!' Ruth gave the chick a sticker. 'Ten times nine is ninety.'

Ninety miles an hour! Amy was a small brown chicken with puffs of grey feathers round her tummy and very red cheeks. She tried to imagine being ten times bigger than she actually was (although maybe not round the tummy). It would be fun to be able to run really fast, especially if she was being chased by a villain. Normally she had to rely on her wrestling moves.

'Now, next question,' said Ruth. 'Which extinct animal is a chicken distantly related to?'

The chicks waited with bated breath. So did Amy. She had no idea science could be so much fun.

'Is it a) a mammoth, b) a dodo, c) a sabre-toothed tiger or d) a T. rex?' Ruth showed them the slides.

Amy and the chicks fell about laughing. *A T. rex? Ha ha ha! It couldn't be that, or a mammoth, or a sabre-toothed tiger!* The whole class, including Amy, put their wings up confidently for dodo because a dodo was a bird and looked a bit like a chicken except with a bigger beak.

'And the answer is . . .'

Amy and the chicks were on the edge of their seats, waiting to be proved right.

'. . . a T. rex.'

'NO WAY!' Amy and the chicks exploded. The classroom was full of excited chatter.

Ruth waited for calm. 'It's true,' she said, when the din had died down. 'Scientists have proved that chickens are the closest living relatives to the mighty T. rex.' She put the slide of the enormous dinosaur up for the class to have another look at. Amy had never seen such a scary-looking monster. She couldn't imagine how a chicken could be related to it in any way. Luckily none of her family back at Perrin's Farm looked anything like that!

'So, you see, chicks, that's two scientific reasons

why us chickens are pretty cool,' Ruth concluded.

Everyone chirped in agreement. Just then the bell went. The hen-mistress of Dudley Coop Academy stood up. She had been sitting in on the lesson as well. She made her way to the front of the class and presented Ruth with a bunch of freshly picked dandelions. 'I'm sure we'd all like to thank Ruth for giving up her time today and coming in to teach us such amazing facts about chickens,' she said. 'Let's give her a big round of applause.' The classroom erupted into wild clapping and cheering.

Ruth looked embarrassed.

Amy joined in the noise. She was pleased for her friend. Ruth's special skill was intelligence and it was nice for her to have the opportunity to share some of it with the chicks. Actually, thinking about it, her *own* special skill was courage. Amy wondered if the hen-mistress would let her come and give the chicks a wrestling lesson one day? She must remember to ask.

'Now, it's break time.' The hen-mistress led the way out of the coop.

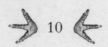

The chicks rushed outside in a jolly throng to play on the grass.

Amy scuttled over to Ruth and gave her a pat on the back. 'That was brilliant!' she said. 'I wish I'd had a science teacher like you when I was at school!'

'Thanks, Amy,' Ruth said, collecting her books. 'It was nice of you to come and watch.'

'It's a pity Boo couldn't be here too,' Amy said. 'She'd have loved it.' Boo was the third member of the elite-chicken squad. She was very good at gymnastics and her special skill was perseverance.

'I know,' said Ruth. 'But someone had to stay behind at Chicken HQ in case the professor called for us.'

Chicken HQ was where the three chickens lived. It was hidden away from the humans in some dilapidated potting sheds in the old walled vegetable garden of Dudley Manor, a short distance beyond the chicken coops.

'I wish the professor *would* call for us,' Amy said wistfully. 'It's been ages since our last mission.'

'That's a good thing, if you think about it,' Ruth

reminded her. 'It might even mean that we've got rid of Thaddeus E. Fox once and for all.'

'I doubt it,' Amy said. Thaddeus E. Fox was the chickens' mortal enemy. He lived in the Deep Dark Woods next to the Dudley Estate and, together with other members of the MOST WANTED Club, dedicated his life to making foxy plans to catch and eat chickens.

'Well, he hasn't been seen for ages by any of the professor's bird spies,' Ruth said.

'Maybe he's gone on holiday,' Amy replied a little glumly. She never thought she'd miss Thaddeus E. Fox, but it had to be said that life at Chicken HQ was a smidgeon dull without him around.

'Why don't you read one of my books if you're bored?' Ruth suggested. 'They're full of interesting facts. And you never know when they might come in handy.'

'Maybe,' said Amy. She wasn't very good at reading. She picked up one of the books and flicked through it. 'What's this one about?' she asked curiously. It had lots of diagrams of skeletons in it.

'The evolution of birds,' Ruth said.

Amy looked blank. 'What's ev-o-lu-shun?' she asked.

'Evolution is the scientific study of where things come from and how they've changed over time,' Ruth told her. 'This book is about how birds have evolved over millions of years.'

'Oh,' said Amy.

Ruth was warming to her theme. 'For example, some scientists believe that birds are a type of dinosaur. They say that birds are actually the only dinosaurs left on earth. That's where I got the information about us being related to the T. rex,' she added.

'Wow!' said Amy. She was beginning to feel muddled. *Did that mean she was a dinosaur as well as a chicken?* Unlike Ruth she only had a tiny brain.

She was just about to ask her friend when the door to the classroom burst open. A beautiful chicken with thick honey-coloured feathers down to her toes rushed in. It was Boo. 'Quick, you two,' she said, 'you've got to return to Chicken HQ.'

'Why, what's happened?' asked Amy, passing the

book back to Ruth. She'd already forgotten all about dinosaurs. Her heart was beating fast with excitement.

'Professor Rooster's just called,' said Boo. 'He's got another mission for us.'

Chapter Two

The chickens squeezed through a hole in the wall of the vegetable garden and dashed up the path to the potting sheds. There were three sheds in total. From the outside they looked as if they were all separate, but inside the potting sheds had been joined together to make one big space.

Amy pushed open the first of the three green doors and hurried through. At one end of the sheds was the chickens' sleeping quarters and a birdbath. At the other end was the gadgets cupboard. And in the middle, on an upturned wooden crate, was a laptop.

The laptop was how Professor Rooster communicated with the chickens. He lived in a secret location and never came to Chicken HQ. In fact, the chickens had met him only once, when they'd rescued him from being kidnapped by Thaddeus E. Fox and his gang during their second mission.

The chickens gathered round the computer. Each

of them had a small garden stool to sit on. Amy scrambled onto hers and promptly fell off again, she was so excited.

'Whoops!' Boo extended a strong wing towards her.

Amy took it gratefully. When they had first met during their training at the International School of Kung Fu for Poultry, thousands of miles away in Tibet, Amy had been a bit in awe of Boo and Ruth. But now she never felt embarrassed in front of them, even when she did something silly like fall off a garden stool. They were a team and they watched out for one another, which is why the elite-chicken squad had been such a success. She heaved herself back onto the stool with Boo's help and got comfortable.

'Ah, there you are, Amy!' A stern-faced black cockerel with a scarlet comb stared out at them from the screen.

'Hello, Professor.' Amy gave him a wave. The screen was two-way so that the professor could see them too.

The professor's stern expression didn't change

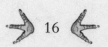

but his eyes twinkled. He had grown fond of the chickens, especially Amy, but he liked to keep things professional and make sure they followed instructions.

'Sorry to keep you waiting, Professor,' Ruth said. 'I was giving the month 4 chicks a science lesson.'

'I know,' said the professor. 'Boo told me. And if I may say so, I think it's an excellent way to spend your spare time. Although you won't have much of that over the next few days.'

'Is it another mission, Professor?' Amy squawked.

'Yes.' The professor's face became even more serious and the twinkle in his eye disappeared as he got down to business. 'And I can tell you that you're going to need all the scientific knowledge you have, Ruth, if the team is to succeed again.'

'In what way, Professor?' asked Ruth, puzzled.

'I'll explain in a minute. First, let me introduce you to one of the most evil villains known to chickens . . .'

'Not Thaddeus E. Fox?' Amy interrupted.

The professor silenced her with a look. 'No, not Thaddeus,' he said shortly. 'This creature's much worse.'

The chickens glanced at one another. *Much worse than Thaddeus? They must be really bad.*

The professor had disappeared from the screen. His image was replaced by a picture of the most ferocious-looking bird Amy had ever seen. It was incredibly tall with brown-and-beige spotted feathers, and a sort of fluffy, striped chest. Its face was round and outlined with a rim of black, and its head was topped off by two feathery tufts as big as a cat's ears. It had piercing, bright orange eyes, which seemed to stare straight at you, and its beak and talons looked sharp enough to slice through chicken wire.

'It's an eagle owl,' Ruth whispered.

'Indeed it is, Ruth,' the professor's voice confirmed, 'but not just *any* eagle owl. This is Vladimir Alexei Raptorov, the world's most intelligent bird. Also known as Vlad the Impaler thanks to his unpleasant habit of skewering his victims through the heart with his talons and nibbling the meat off them like a kebab.'

Amy swallowed.

'In case you're wondering, he also has a two-metre wingspan, binocular night vision and can hear the drop of a pin from twenty metres away. Oh, and did I mention his favourite food is chicken?'

Amy listened carefully. She knew better than to interrupt even though she had loads of questions she wanted to ask.

'Like I say, Raptorov isn't any ordinary bird,' the professor continued. 'He was bred in captivity to be used by the humans for their scientific experiments, hence his love of chicken. That's what the humans fed him, you see.'

'What kind of experiments?' asked Ruth, as the slideshow moved to a picture of Raptorov tethered to

a perch in a laboratory. He was tearing into a chicken leg surrounded by humans in white coats.

'Genetic engineering,' the professor replied.

'Oh,' said Ruth, apparently taken aback.

Amy and Boo glanced at one another. 'What's genetic engineering?' Amy mouthed.

Boo shrugged. 'Search me!' she whispered.

Amy stuck her wing up boldly. 'Please, Professor, could you tell me and Boo what that is?'

'Certainly,' said the professor. He scratched his comb. 'Hmm, now how can I put it simply?'

'Perhaps I can help, Professor,' Ruth said. She turned to her friends. 'Genetic engineering is the process of adding one animal's DNA to another animal to change it.'

Amy didn't feel any the wiser. 'What's DNA?' she asked.

'It's the teeny tiny stuff in our bodies that makes us what we are,' Ruth said. 'It's what gives Boo honey-coloured feathers and me bad eyesight, and Amy red cheeks.'

Amy screwed up her face in concentration. She was

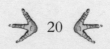

determined to keep up with what Ruth was saying even if it stretched her little chicken brain to the limit!

'Okay,' said Boo slowly, 'so what's the point of giving one animal's DNA to another?'

'Well, going back to an example I used this morning in class, say that chickens wanted to run faster than humans, one way to do it would be to give chickens the DNA of a really fast animal like a cheetah,' Ruth explained.

Aha! Amy thought she'd cracked it. 'So if chickens wanted to be really fierce, you could give them the DNA of a T. rex?' she suggested brightly.

'Well, yes, except that dinosaurs died out sixty million years ago,' Ruth replied, 'so that wouldn't actually be possible. But you've definitely got the right idea, Amy.'

Amy felt pleased with herself. She was really getting the hang of science thanks to Ruth.

'Thank you, Ruth. That was very well explained,' the professor said. He cleared his throat. 'The point is, chickens, that Raptorov has been genetically modified by the humans. He is smarter than any other

bird on the planet. That's how he escaped from the laboratory. He also has stronger wings, sharper talons, better eyesight and better hearing than any other owl in the world, and that's saying something.'

'Does he have any weaknesses?' asked Boo.

'Not really,' the professor said. 'Although he does have a love of Russian classical music, particularly the works of Tchaikovsky. I believe it sends him into a sort of trance.'

'So, where do we come in?' asked Amy. She decided to ask the others who Tchaikovsky was later. She didn't want the professor to think she was completely stupid!

'Raptorov has been spotted by my bird spies hovering above the beach at Stormy Cliff Caravan Park, about forty miles north from here as the crow flies,' the professor replied. 'He's hiding out in some caves on a nearby island. The caravan park is home to a large flock of chickens. They are largely unprotected by humans. So far Raptorov hasn't launched an attack on them, which is surprising. But he will, I'm sure of it. Your mission is to stop him.'

'Don't worry, Professor, you can rely on us!' Amy said, punching the air. She knew she should be afraid, but actually she couldn't wait to get started. The mission sounded ace. 'Have you got any good gadgets for us?'

Professor Rooster always provided them with useful things in times of chicken crisis (although how he sneaked them into Chicken HQ remained a complete mystery).

'Er, yes, there are some in the Emergency Chicken Pack,' the professor said. For some reason he seemed a little distracted.

Amy wondered what was wrong. Normally the professor just switched off the monitor and let them get on with it, but it seemed as if there was something else he wanted to say. She waited.

Professor Rooster gave a little cough. 'Er . . . the thing is, chickens,' he began apologetically, 'it's vital that this mission succeeds. If Raptorov isn't stopped, no chicken anywhere in the land will be safe. That's why I . . . er . . . think you might need a bit of help . . . some-birdy experienced . . .'

Help? The three chickens looked at one another in alarm. *He didn't mean . . . ??? He couldn't . . . ???? Not . . . ?????*

'So I called up Poultry Patrol and asked for their best agent . . .' said the professor more briskly.

NOOOOOOOOOOOOOOOOOOOOOOO!!!!!!!!! Amy felt like screaming.

'. . . and they're sending James Pond. He'll be with you in about an hour. Good luck.' The professor leaned forward and switched off the monitor. The screen fizzled for a minute and then went black.

Chapter Three

'I can't believe Professor Rooster would do this to us!' Amy fumed.

'James Pond, of all birds!' muttered Boo.

'I can't stand that duck,' sighed Ruth. 'He's such a show-off.'

The chickens stomped round Chicken HQ preparing for their mission. Ruth was assembling the gadgets, Boo was preparing some food for the journey and Amy was, well, just stomping round.

'And he's useless!' she huffed, her cheeks blazing. 'Every time he's supposed to help us he ends up getting gummed by zombie chickens, or tricked by cunning foxes or hypnotised by cobras.'

'I know,' Boo said, slamming the mini-fridge door. 'It's us who have to help *him*, not the other way around!'

'He does have some good gadgets though,' said Ruth, rummaging about in her cupboard. 'I suppose *they* might come in handy, even if he doesn't.'

'I suppose,' said Amy crossly. She stomped over to the laptop. 'Anyone mind if I have a quick game of Chicken World Wrestling 6 before he arrives?' she asked. 'Only I need to let off some steam.'

'Go ahead,' said Ruth.

'Be my guest,' agreed Boo.

'Thanks.' Amy loaded the game. The contestants were based on famous real-life chicken wrestling

champions and the first thing she had to do was choose who she wanted to be. That was easy! Amy picked Rocky Termin-egger – her favourite fighter of all time. The next screen gave her a choice of opponents. Amy hummed and haaaed before finally plumping for Granny Wishbone. Granny Wishbone was Chicken World Wrestling's dirtiest fighter, which meant Amy didn't feel at all guilty when she beat her in the game.

The bell went. 'Start of round one!' said the commentator. Rocky bounced into the ring and showed off his muscly wings. Before Amy could do anything about it Granny Wishbone had snuck under the wire while his back was turned and bashed him on the head with her zimmer frame. Rocky passed out.

'End of round one!' said the commentator.

'Okay,' said Amy, taking a long, slow breath, 'you've asked for it, Wishbone.'

'Start of round two!'

This time Rocky went for a winglock but Granny Wishbone was too quick for him. She spun out of his grasp and pinned his neck to the ground with her

false teeth. The referee counted him out.

'End of round two!'

'Okay, Wishbone,' snarled Amy, 'this is war.' Her cheeks sizzled.

'Start of round three!'

Rocky dived for Granny Wishbone's scrawny legs. Granny Wishbone lashed out with a karate kick. Then she wheeled round and elbowed Rocky in the face with her bony elbow, knocking him unconscious for the second time.

'Fowl!' shrieked the crowd (and Amy). But the referee hadn't seen.

'End of round three!' shouted the commentator. 'Granny Wishbone wins!'

'Oh, honestly!' Amy switched off the computer. Playing Chicken World Wrestling 6 wasn't helping very much. She felt crosser than ever.

'Come and help me with the gadgets, Amy,' said Ruth. 'I need to check them off against my list.'

'Okay.' Amy scuttled over.

'Flight booster engines . . .'

'Check!'

'Infra-red super-spec headsets with advanced radar tracking . . .'

'Check!'

'Mite blaster . . .'

'Check!'

'Evil baddie Geiger counter . . .'

'What's that?' asked Amy. She knew all about the other gadgets because they had used them on their previous missions, but she'd never heard of the evil baddie Geiger counter.

'It looks like a watch,' Ruth said, 'but instead of picking up high levels of radiation like a normal Geiger counter does, it picks up high levels of evil baddie activity, so you can tell where they are and their evilness level even if you can't actually see them.'

'That's brilliant!' Amy said. 'Was it in the Emergency Chicken Pack?'

'Actually, it's something I invented,' Ruth said modestly. 'I think it might come in handy against Raptorov because he's so difficult to detect.'

'It's a great idea,' said Amy, picking up the 'watch'

and trying it on for size. It had a white face with a red needle and a dial calibrated in units from one to ten.

'Zero means no baddie activity detected, ten means it's as evil as it can get,' Ruth explained.

'So where would Thaddeus be on this?' Boo asked, coming over to have a look.

'I'd say he'd be about a five,' Ruth said. 'Raptorov's probably an eight from what the professor says.'

'What about the MOST WANTED Club?'

'Put together with Thaddeus maybe about the same as Raptorov – an eight. Individually they're probably only a one though, and that's counting the pigeons as a group. They don't have the same capacity for evil as Thaddeus and Raptorov unless they have help.'

'Oh,' said Amy. The other members of the MOST WANTED Club were Tiny Tony Tiddles, a black and white cat with a gangster hat, Kebab Claude, a large French poodle with a love of cooking barbecues, and the Pigeon-Poo Gang, three nasty birds with shades who would do anything for grain and sludged their victims to death with their cement-like poo.

'It's just as well it's only Raptorov we've got to

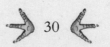

deal with this time,' Ruth joked, 'or I'd have to put more numbers on the dial!'

'It's really clever, Ruth,' Boo said, taking the device from Amy and trying it on. 'Only I wish you'd made the strap purple!' Purple was Boo's favourite colour.

'Call that a gadget?' quacked a snooty voice from the doorway. 'No wonder the professor asked me to help.' A large mallard duck stepped into the potting sheds. He was wearing a bow tie and had a holster strapped under his left wing. 'Hello again, hopeless hens! My name is Pond, James Pond.'

'WE KNOW YOUR NAME!' Amy shouted at him. 'AND WE'RE NOT HOPELESS!' She kicked the floor and stubbed her toe painfully in the process. 'Ow!'

'You sure about that?' James Pond sniggered.

'You should have invented an annoying big-head Geiger counter, Ruth,' Boo remarked coolly, returning the machine to her friend, 'except he'd probably break it.'

Amy giggled in spite of her sore toe. She wished she'd thought of something clever like that to say!

'Very funny,' said James Pond. '*Not!* Now who wants to see *my* gadgets?'

'I do,' said Ruth.

Actually Amy secretly did too. 'Okay,' she said in what she hoped was an uninterested voice.

James Pond waddled towards them. He fiddled with his bow tie. The knot in the centre projected a beam of bright white light towards them. The chickens turned away, covering their eyes with their wings.

'It's a laser torch,' James Pond explained. 'Raptorov is nocturnal, that's why he's hanging out in the caves at

Stormy Island. This will render him temporarily dazed.'
He switched off the torch. The chickens blinked. They
were still half blinded by the dazzling light.

'What else?' asked Ruth, taking off her specs and
rubbing her eyes.

'A homing device.' This time James Pond reached
for his holster. He drew out a long slim box. It bore
the label:

IGOR'S
EAGLE OWL
HOMING DEVICE

'Here!' He handed it to Ruth. She opened it
carefully while Amy and Boo looked on curiously.
The box contained a tightly packed nylon net, several
corks, a pair of pliers and a thin strip of metal with a
blank electronic display.

Ruth unfolded the instructions and read them out
loud.

Worried in case your eagle owl escapes? Then Igor's eagle owl homing device is for you! Developed from genuine Russian missile technology, this brilliant invention will ensure that your eagle owl never strays again!

<u>Instructions</u>
Stun eagle owl with laser torch (not included).
Trap bird with net.
Set required coordinates on homing device.
Attach to eagle owl's leg using pliers.
Remove net.

NB: For extra protection against being skewered through the heart, attach corks to eagle owl's talons.
Results guaranteed!

'All we have to do is set the co-ordinates on the homing device to the Russian laboratory where Raptorov came from, fix it on to his leg with the pliers and off he goes,' James Pond explained. 'The missile technology will force him to go back there even if he doesn't want to. Whichever way he flaps, that's where he'll end up.'

'That's pretty clever,' Ruth admitted.

'Yeah, not bad,' Boo nodded.

Amy didn't say anything. It was pretty clever *IF IT WORKED*! The problem with all James Pond's amazing gadgets was that something unforeseen usually happened to stop him using them.

'Now hurry up. We need to get going.' James Pond went outside to limber up ready for take-off.

Amy let out a deep sigh. Now the duck was involved, this was going to be hard work! But the chickens of Stormy Cliff Caravan Park were depending on them. Whatever she thought about James Pond she knew it mustn't get in the way of the mission.

'Amy, can you bring the Emergency Chicken Pack?' Ruth said, frantically stuffing the remaining gadgets into her backpack along with her book about the evolution of birds.

'Okay.' Amy grabbed it from another cupboard. She wondered what Professor Rooster had put in it this time, and if they would need it.

'I've got the picnic,' Boo said, hurrying over.

The chickens strapped on their flight booster engines and scuttled out into the garden. James Pond was already airborne. He circled above them, his neck outstretched, his wings beating in elegant strokes. One after the other the chickens took off after him from the old walled garden and zoomed up into the sky.

Chapter Four

Down in a burrow in the Deep Dark Woods,
Thaddeus E. Fox cowered under a blanket in a pair
of scruffy pyjamas, waiting for the doctor to arrive.

'Hello?' came a voice in the tunnel. 'Are you there,
Thaddeus? It's Doctor Brush.'

Thaddeus didn't reply. He wriggled deeper under
the bedclothes.

There was a soft *thunk* as the doctor put his bag
down on the floor and tiptoed over. 'Thaddeus?'
The edge of the blanket lifted to reveal the doctor's
face. He was an elderly fox with grey whiskers and a
sensible countenance. His expression was concerned.
'I've brought you another pack of dog biscuits.' He
reached for his bag. 'I'll get them, shall I?'

Thaddeus grabbed him by the stethoscope. 'You
sure you weren't followed, doctor?' he demanded in
a hoarse whisper.

'Quite sure,' said the doctor soothingly.

'And you definitely didn't see any chickens?'

'Definitely,' the doctor reassured him. 'No chickens.'

'What about roosters?'

'Nope, none of them either.' The doctor gently removed his stethoscope from Thaddeus's grasp. 'How about you come out from there and tell me how you've been getting on? There's a good fellow.' He took out the packet of dog biscuits and held them towards his emaciated patient.

Little by little Thaddeus E. Fox removed the blanket from over his head and wrapped it around his thin shoulders. He sucked in an unsteady breath and reached for the dog biscuits with trembling paws.

'Let me,' the doctor said, ripping open the cardboard lid. He took out a dog biscuit and folded Thaddeus's paw around it carefully.

'Thank you,' Thaddeus said meekly. It still took several attempts to get the biscuit into his mouth. When he finally managed it, the fox chomped on the biscuit mechanically. He made no attempt to wipe away the slobber running down his chin.

The doctor regarded his patient with professional curiosity. Clearly there had been no improvement since his last visit. In fact he had been treating Thaddeus E. Fox for some months now and despite his best endeavours, his patient's condition had steadily got worse. If it weren't for him bringing dog biscuits every week Thaddeus would have starved to death by now. The poor animal seemed to have lost his appetite for life entirely.

Thaddeus finished chomping. 'I had another flashback last night,' he whispered, staring into space.

'Ah,' said the doctor sympathetically. 'Was it the one where Professor Rooster's elite-chicken squad humiliated you in front of all your foxy friends from Eat'em College for Gentlemen Foxes?'

'No.' Thaddeus shook his head slowly. 'It was worse.'

'Not the one where you ended up wallowing in cow's muck and spoiling your beautiful clothes?' said the doctor with renewed concern. That elite-chicken squad had a lot to answer for, he thought indignantly. Spoiling an Old Eatemian's clothes was contemptible behaviour. The cow's muck episode was enough to give anyone nightmares!

Thaddeus started trembling all over. 'No,' he hissed. 'It was the other one.'

'What, the one where they launched an aerial bombardment of brick-egg bombs on your head?'

Thaddeus nodded dumbly. He rubbed his head as if it were still throbbing.

The doctor decided to change tack. 'Have you

been out since my last visit?' he said briskly, although he already knew the answer.

'I can't,' Thaddeus moaned. 'They might be lying in wait for me.' He started to sob.

'Now, now,' said the doctor, offering him a handkerchief.

Thaddeus blew his nose loudly. He looked at the doctor pleadingly. 'What's wrong with me, doctor?' he said in a pathetic voice.

The doctor sighed. 'I've told you before, Thaddeus, you have an advanced case of alektorophobia, otherwise known as the fear of chickens.'

Thaddeus gave an involuntary shudder. 'No!' he shook his head vehemently. 'I can't have. I'm a fox! Foxes aren't scared of chickens.' He gripped the doctor's paw. 'It must be something else!'

Oh dear, thought the doctor, his patient was still in denial. Every time he'd visited the burrow he'd told Thaddeus what was wrong with him, but the poor fellow couldn't seem to get to grips with it. He decided to adopt a firmer approach. 'Look here, Thaddeus, unless you face up to what's actually

wrong with you, you'll never get better,' he said crisply.

Thaddeus remained silent.

The doctor felt encouraged. His patient seemed to be listening for a change. He pressed on. 'No one thinks the worse of you for what's happened, Thaddeus. None of your old Eat'em College pals, not me, not even the former members of the MOST WANTED Club.'

'You've seen them?' Thaddeus looked shocked.

'They came to see me, actually,' the doctor said. 'They were worried when they heard what had happened with the brick-eggs bombs.'

'They were?'

'Yes. They wanted to visit you, but I said you weren't well enough.' He patted Thaddeus's paw. 'The fact is, my friend, those chickens have treated you shamefully. They've lost sight of the natural order of things. Any fox in your paws would have ended up the same way. Everyone knows that.'

'You think?' Thaddeus said. There was a touch of hope in his voice.

'I promise you.' The doctor saw he might be getting somewhere at last. He decided to play his trump card. 'Look, Thaddeus, this . . . er . . . condition of yours, I'll be honest – it's a little bit out of my league.' Normally the doctor spent his time amongst the woodland animals treating coughs and sneezes, removing ticks and giving advice to ferrets about how to rear their young. The most exciting it got was setting the occasional badger's broken leg. 'I can't help you. That's why I think you should go and see a specialist: someone who knows how to treat phobias like the one you're suffering from.'

'You mean leave the burrow?' Thaddeus gasped. 'I can't!'

'Now, hear me out,' the doctor said firmly. 'I've found somewhere: a place where the doctors understand your sort of illness; a place full of distressed foxes like you; a place where they can make you better,' the doctor rushed on. 'It's by the sea. Imagine that, Thaddeus! I can almost smell the fresh air!' The doctor twitched his nose. The burrow smelled like an old nappy.

'Fresh air!' Thaddeus let out a little whimper of joy at the thought. Then his face fell. 'I'm not going on my own. I can't! What if they're out there?'

'You don't have to go on your own,' the doctor said patiently. 'I'll come with you and drop you off. We can catch the goods train from Dudley. No one will see us. And it's only a couple of miles across country to the clinic at the other end. Professor Rooster's elite-chicken squad won't even know you've gone! What do you say?'

Thaddeus E. Fox thought for a moment. 'The doctors at the clinic, they'll cure me, you say?'

'Yes,' said the doctor.

'And then I'll be back to my normal evil self?'

'I give you my word.'

Thaddeus let out a long, rasping sigh. 'Okay, I'll go.'

'Excellent!' The doctor jumped up. 'I'll pack a bag for you. Where's your top hat?'

'In the closet with my cane,' Thaddeus responded listlessly. He got up and put his slippers on. Then he shuffled towards the part of the burrow which he

used as a toilet. 'By the way, doctor,' he called, 'what's the name of this place that you're taking me to?'

The doctor threw the last bits and pieces into the bag and snapped it shut. He consulted his notes. 'The Stormy Cliff Convalescent Home for Distressed Foxes,' he replied. 'Now, hurry up or we'll miss that train!'

Chapter Five

Meanwhile, to the north, the chickens were making good progress. The weather was fine and they had covered the distance quickly from Dudley Manor to the countryside near Stormy Cliff. It was only when they struck out for the coast that they started to experience difficulties. The sea breeze was so strong and gusty that it buffeted them backwards and forwards. It was all they could do to keep a straight course.

James Pond had no such problems. He might be ungainly on land, but he was a good flyer. Amy felt envious. She wished chickens could fly without flight booster engines. Maybe someone should give them some of that DNA stuff from a different bird like an albatross!

Amy flew on. They were nearly at the coast. She could see where the land ended and fell away into the sea. Amy had never been to the seaside before.

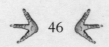

Although it was a sunny day, the sea looked cold and uninviting. She couldn't ever imagine wanting to swim in it, even if she could actually stay afloat without her feathers getting waterlogged. Swimming was another thing James Pond could do and chickens couldn't. It wasn't fair!

'There's the caravan park!' Boo shouted. The three chickens were flying in a line behind James Pond; Boo first, then Amy, with Ruth bringing up the rear. They were trying to stay in the duck agent's slipstream so they didn't have to use up so much energy.

Amy looked down. Beneath them, set back from the cliff face, were two rows of rickety old caravans at right angles to the sea. At the end of the park was a field full of tiny brown specks. *The chicken flock!*

'And there's Stormy Island!' Up ahead, a little way out to sea, a great chunk of pale grey rock loomed out of the water like a gigantic tombstone.

'The three friends reduced their speed, expecting to fly over the field where the other chickens lived, but to their dismay James Pond flew over the caravans and on towards the island.

'What are you doing?' Ruth shouted after him.

'I want to get the lie of the land while Raptorov's asleep,' James Pond quacked. 'We need to find the way into the caves.'

Amy felt exhausted. All she wanted to do was go and meet the other chickens and get some decent grub. 'Can't we wait until tomorrow?' she called hopefully.

'No,' James Pond shouted. 'There's no time to lose.'

'He's right, Amy.' Boo flew alongside her. 'The professor said Raptorov could attack at any time. The sooner we find out where he lives, the better.'

Amy nodded despondently. Teatime with the chickens of Stormy Cliff would have to wait.

On they flew over the edge of the cliff. Amy glanced back. The cliff face was the same colour as the island – greyish white. It wasn't quite the sheer drop she had imagined, though. A steep path led down to the beach through a tangle of windblown bushes. The beach itself stretched as far as she could see in both directions. The part closest to the cliff was strewn with boulders where the cliff had fallen away. Next to it was a strip of dry white sand, which became darker and wetter the further you looked out to sea.

'The tide's out,' Ruth explained, coming alongside her. 'Look! There's the causeway.'

'Oh yes!' said Amy. A thin path of slippery-looking rock led across the sea from the beach to the island. Even at low tide it didn't look very safe.

'We'll put down at the end of the causeway,' James Pond instructed. 'And remember, no one make a sound.'

The causeway came to an end at a small patch of shingle. The chickens started their descent. Amy could hear the hiss of stones as the sea swept in and out against the shingle.

James Pond came in to land. He raised his upper body, beating his wings against the air to slow him down and dropped neatly onto the sea. From there he paddled to the shingle bank.

The chickens landed with some difficulty beside him. Amy had particular problems. Maybe it was

because she was smaller than the others, or because her tummy was fluffier, but although the sun was still shining strongly the wind seemed to catch her feathers and toss her around like a balloon. Eventually she managed to set down, landing with a loud crunch on her knees on the gravel.

'Ouch!' The yelp of pain escaped from her beak before she had a chance to stop it.

James Pond shot her a filthy look. Boo and Ruth raised their wings to their beaks to shush her. Amy hung her head. If Raptorov could hear the drop of a pin from twenty metres away, then he could certainly hear a chicken squawk if he was anywhere close. She hoped she hadn't jeopardised the mission.

The four birds waited anxiously. Eventually James Pond gave a nod to signal that he thought it was safe to go on. Amy breathed a sigh of relief. Raptorov must be asleep somewhere deep inside the caves, hiding away from the bright sunshine. He hadn't heard her after all.

James Pond hopped up onto the rocks, beckoning the chickens to follow him. Amy fluttered up

unsteadily beside him. There was no sign of the cave entrance. In fact there wasn't a crack to be seen in the sheer rock face. This was going to be harder than they thought.

James Pond set off at a quick pace along the rocks that ringed the island. It was all right for him, Amy thought wearily as she slipped and slithered after her friends in a wonky line. The duck's big webbed feet meant he could keep his balance. It wasn't that easy if you had chicken toes, unless you were Boo, of course, who had no trouble at all with the smooth, wet surface because of her gymnastics training.

On they hopped from boulder to boulder. After a little while, when Amy thought she couldn't possibly cling on any longer, they arrived at a long, low ledge. Behind it, worn away by the sea, was the mouth of a cave!

Amy peered in. It was quite dark inside, but she could see that the floor was littered with more stones. The stones were the same greyish white as the cliff. Some of them had been split open. They seemed to have strange patterns carved on them. Ruth was

staring at them intently, a puzzled expression on her face. Amy wondered why.

Boo gave Ruth a nudge and pointed to her backpack.

Ruth nodded. Silently she removed the evil baddie Geiger counter and fixed it onto her wing. She tiptoed into the mouth of the cave and held her wing outstretched for a few seconds. Then she tiptoed back. She held out the gadget so that the others could see.

The dial registered a score of eight.

Raptorov! They had found the entrance to his lair.

Suddenly Amy felt terrified. What if the owl was watching them from somewhere in the darkness with his binocular eyes? What if he really *had* heard her squawk? What if he suddenly flew out and skewered them with his great talons? Would he really be put off by the bright sunshine? She wasn't so sure now. She felt her strength ebb. The journey had taken it out of her. She was cold and wet and tired and very hungry.

Suddenly Amy's tummy let out an enormous grumble. It echoed round the cave like a clap of thunder. *Oh no! She'd done it again!*

This time she was answered by a noise from somewhere inside the island, beyond the cave.

'HVRECK! HVRECK!'

Amy had never heard a sound like it. It was somewhere between a bark and a scream.

'Raptorov!' James Pond hissed. 'You've woken him up this time. Quick! We need to get out of here before he sees us.'

The duck waddled out onto the ledge and ran along it, his wings beating furiously. He caught an updraft of wind and launched himself into the air.

The three chickens scuttled onto the ledge after him.

Boo and Ruth put their flight boosters to ROCKET BLAST MAX and zoomed off in the direction of Stormy Cliff. Amy fumbled with her controls. Her wings were slippery from all the sea spray and she felt so worn out she could hardly think straight.

'HVRECK! HVRECK!' The sound was getting closer. Raptorov was coming! Amy raised her head. A huge, hunched shadow stretched across the cave. It had the shape of a vampire in a horror movie,

only it was much, much bigger. Raptorov must be approaching the cave from a tunnel. And, judging by the way his shadow was growing, it was only a matter of seconds before he emerged.

Help!!!! Amy made her waterlogged wings into fists and gripped the control with all her might. Somehow she forced the knob to the right setting. *Click!* Amy felt herself lift straight up high into the air, close to the face of the cliff. She glanced down,

half expecting to see the owl take off from the ledge after her and give chase. But there was no sign of Raptorov. He was either waiting in the cave or had gone back to his lair to resume his sleep.

Amy hovered for what seemed an age. Then, when she felt it was safe she shot off towards Stormy Cliff after her friends.

Chapter Six

About an hour later, Amy was feeling much better. She was sitting on the step of one of the old caravans that doubled up as the chickens' sleeping quarters, surrounded by a group of admiring chicks. Boo and Ruth were next to her. Most gratifyingly of all, James Pond was nowhere to be seen. As no one had been expecting him, he'd had to be temporarily housed in the old dustbin shed next to the loos.

'Did you actually see Raptorov?' one of the chicks said in awe.

'No, just his shadow,' Amy replied. Suddenly her close shave with death at the talons of Vladimir Alexei Raptorov had turned into an enormous adventure rather than an accident of her own making. 'He was all hunched over. And he was making a horrible noise.'

'That's typical owl behaviour,' Ruth commented. 'When they're on the attack they hunch themselves

forwards and spread their wings to make themselves look bigger. It's known as their threat posture. That's why he was making that noise. He was warning off intruders.'

'I suppose the real question is did Raptorov see *you*?' Boo asked Amy.

Amy had been wondering about that too. If Raptorov *had* seen her she knew it might cause problems for the mission. The sight of a small chicken with a flight booster engine and an infra-red super-spec headset would be bound to make the owl suspicious. 'I don't think so,' she said slowly. 'I took off before he reached the cave. And he didn't try and follow me. I think he went back inside the cliff.'

'Weren't you scared?' asked another chick.

'Nope,' Amy lied. 'Not a bit.' It wasn't exactly boasting. The chicks had faith in the elite-chicken squad; she didn't want to scare *them* by admitting that she had nearly been frightened out of her feathers.

'Do you think you can get rid of him?' A third chick asked in a small voice.

'Well, er . . .' *Actually, could they?* Amy wasn't sure.

Now that she had seen the shadow of the great owl at close range, the idea of stunning him with James Pond's bow-tie laser torch and fitting the homing device onto his leg seemed even more daunting than it had done back at Chicken HQ.

'Of course we can,' Boo said confidently, coming to her rescue. 'We wouldn't be here otherwise.'

'Hooray!' yelled the chicks.

Amy hopped off the steps. She hoped Boo was right. Meanwhile it had turned into a beautiful afternoon. The wind had dropped and now that her tummy was full of chicken feed (generously supplied by her new friends), she felt like doing some exploring. 'Who fancies a trip to the beach?' she said.

'We do!' the chicks cheeped.

'Are you sure it's safe?' one of the mother hens asked anxiously.

Amy looked at Ruth for guidance.

'It should be,' Ruth said. 'Raptorov's nocturnal. He'll only attack at night. Although I'm a bit puzzled as to why he hasn't done so already.'

'We've been sleeping in the caravan,' the hen said.

'Even so . . .' Ruth cast a dubious look at the dilapidated caravan. She didn't say any more, but Amy could tell there was something on her mind.

'Shall we go then?' Amy said brightly. She didn't want the chickens to start worrying that they weren't safe after all, and besides, she really wanted to go to the beach.

The mother hens went into a huddle. 'All right,' they agreed eventually. 'But make sure you're back before it gets dark.'

'Yay!' The chicks scurried off towards the cliff path. Boo and Ruth rushed after them.

Amy was about to follow when one of the mother hens called her back. 'Here!' she said, thrusting a basket over Amy's wing. 'Take this – it's got all the beach stuff in it. And this!' She threw a towel over Amy's other wing.

'Thanks!' Amy raced after the others.

Boo and Ruth were picking their way through the bushes, deep in conversation. 'So what do you think Raptorov's up to?' Boo was asking Ruth in a low voice.

'I wish I knew,' Ruth replied. 'I can't figure it out.'

'What do you mean?' asked Amy, joining her friends. 'Raptorov wants to eat chickens. That's what the professor said. He's like Thaddeus E. Fox, only worse.'

'Ruth doesn't think it's that simple, Amy,' Boo explained, taking the towel from her.

'Why not?'

'Well, if all he wanted to do was eat chickens, why hasn't he attacked the flock already?' Ruth said. 'The caravan wouldn't hold him off for long. Did you see how dilapidated it is? He could easily get in if he tried.'

'But what else *could* he want?' Amy said, flummoxed.

Ruth shook her head. 'I don't know. But I've got a feeling it's something to do with this place. I mean why choose Stormy Island? He could have gone anywhere.' She paused. 'Did you see those stones in the cave?'

Boo nodded. 'I was wondering what they were.'

'Me too,' said Amy. 'I meant to ask you about them. They had carvings on.'

'They weren't carvings,' said Ruth. 'They were fossils.'

'Fossils?' Boo exclaimed.

Amy listened carefully. She knew vaguely what a fossil was. It was the remains of an animal from millions of years ago that had somehow been turned into stone, although how that actually happened she hadn't got a clue! Maybe Ruth knew.

Boo was still speaking. 'What on earth would Raptorov want with fossils?' she said.

'I'm not sure yet,' Ruth sighed. 'But there are loads of them around here. These cliffs are chalk, you see — and chalk is one of the best types of rock to find fossils in. And if he wants them for some reason, this is the place to come.'

Boo looked at her friend incredulously. 'You think that's why he's at Stormy Island?' she said. 'To collect fossils?'

Ruth didn't get a chance to answer because they had arrived at the beach. The chicks dashed about excitedly. Amy was excited too. She felt the soft sand between her toes. It was much less scratchy than dirt.

Amy decided she liked the beach. She thought she might even go for a paddle if the water wasn't too cold!

'Maybe we should organise some games,' Boo suggested, laying the towel out neatly.

'Good idea,' said Amy, setting the basket of beach stuff down. The chicks gathered round.

'Who wants to make sandcastles?' Amy asked, pulling out some plastic ice-cream spoons and tubs that doubled as buckets and spades.

'Me, me, me, me, me!'

Amy handed them out. 'Maybe you should be in charge of that, Ruth?' she suggested.

'All right,' Ruth agreed. 'Let's go where the sand's a bit wetter,' she said in her teacher's voice, 'then we can make a really cool castle with a moat.' She set off towards the darker sand. A group of chicks followed her obediently.

Next to come out of the basket was a bag containing a long net made of string, two lollipop sticks and a bouncy ball. 'Volleyball!' Boo cried. 'Amy, how about you make up one team and I make up the other?'

'Okay.' Amy loved volleyball. She used to play with her friends at Perrin's Farm before she became a chicken warrior.

The two chickens found a patch of flat sand and set up the net. Then they divided the excited chicks into teams with Boo as captain of one team and Amy of the other. Very soon the game was under way.

It proved to be loads of fun. The chicks had bags of energy. They raced around, keeping the ball up in the air with their wings and passing it between them; setting it up for the captains (who were taller) to bash over the net. Boo's team had the advantage as Boo was brilliant at jumping, but Amy didn't mind. What she lacked in height, she made up for in determination. Besides, everyone was enjoying themselves so much, no one was bothering to keep score anyway!

The ball was at Amy's end. *BOUNCE! BOUNCE! BOUNCE!* The chicks worked it steadily towards her while Amy got into position. *BOUNCE!* Her teammate sent the ball high in the air.

Amy bent her knees and jumped up to meet it, stretching out her wing to make the strike.

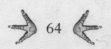

Suddenly Boo gave a shout. 'Watch out behind you!' she yelled.

Amy wondered what on earth was the matter. Then she remembered Raptorov. Had he decided to attack in daylight after all? She turned her head, fearing the worst. But instead of the eagle owl, Amy saw a wizened old chicken hurtling through the air towards her with a horrible war-like expression on its face. A second later a sharp elbow connected with her head as the chicken knocked her out of the way, intercepted the ball and whacked it over the net with its tatty wings.

'OOF!' Amy plunged to the ground, seeing stars.

'HEE-HEE-HEE!' the chicken screeched, landing on top of her in a scrawny heap. 'Good strike, grannies. Someone pass me my zimmer frame.'

Grannies??? Zimmer frame??? Amy could hardly believe her ears. She dragged herself out from under her attacker so she could get a better look. A group of ancient hens had gathered beside the volleyball pitch, cackling encouragement. As for their ringleader, Amy knew exactly who *she* was.

'Granny Wishbone!' she said crossly. 'It's you!'

The dirtiest fighter in Chicken World Wrestling staggered to her feet, her sallow chicken skin sagging around her ankles. 'In the flesh,' she replied triumphantly, removing her false teeth and showering Amy with sandy spit.

Amy brushed it off in disgust. 'But what on earth are you doing here, of all places?' she demanded.

'It's the annual Granny Hen Beach Volleyball Championships. We're staying at the caravan park for the weekend.' Granny Wishbone's face assumed an

even meaner expression. She addressed her ancient cronies. 'Who wants to jump on some sandcastles?'

A cheer went up from the granny hens. They raised their zimmer frames in salute and scuttled off towards where Ruth and the other chicks had been hard at work.

Amy let out a deep sigh. Working with James Pond was bad enough, but having to put up with Granny Wishbone and her gummy granny pals was even worse. This mission was turning out to be a pain in the gizzard.

Chapter Seven

Not far away, at the Stormy Cliff Convalescent Home for Distressed Foxes, Thaddeus E. Fox was getting accustomed to his new surroundings. The doctor had gone back to the Deep Dark Woods to deliver more baby ferrets, leaving Thaddeus in the care of the specialist fox-iatric team.

He was beginning to feel a bit better. It was good to have a change of scene. Being surrounded by other afflicted and recovering foxes helped. So did knowing that Professor Rooster and his elite-chicken squad would never find him here in a million years. He was safe.

In fact, Thaddeus didn't think he'd ever been anywhere so remote in his life. The convalescent home was in a derelict stone farmhouse set high above the sea on the clifftop. Like most other places on Stormy Cliff, the farmhouse had long been abandoned by the humans, but in this case the roof was still sound and the walls were reasonably weather-proof. Thaddeus had been given a small room in the attic. It lacked the earthy cosiness of his burrow but had a reassuringly pungent, foxy smell from its previous occupants. The mattress wasn't as comfortable as his own feather bed at home either – it was rather thin, like him, and its springs dug into his ribs – but it would do. For the first time in ages Thaddeus felt optimistic. He had high hopes for the Stormy Cliff Convalescent Home. He wanted to be cured.

The one thing the attic room did have was a good view. Thaddeus gazed out of the window. Dusk was gathering, but it was still light enough to see that the empty shore along Stormy Cliff stretched for miles in both directions. Nor was there anything visible on the horizon except a small island a little way to the north, which stuck out of the sea like a gigantic tombstone. He opened the window and leaned out to get a better look. He caught sight of a dilapidated caravan park, which stood on the cliff opposite the island. It looked as if the humans had abandoned that as well.

Just then there was a knock at the door. 'Mr Fox?'
It was one of the nurses.

'Yes.'

'It's time for your therapy session.'

'Coming,' Thaddeus said jauntily. He closed the
window and trotted down the stairs after the nurse.

The therapy session was held in what had once been
the farmhouse kitchen. Half a dozen foxes sat round
the room in a rough semicircle in front of an unlit
iron stove. Facing them was one of the fox-iatrists.

'I'm Doctor Thicket,' she said to Thaddeus.
'Welcome.'

Thaddeus's optimism began to evaporate. He didn't
feel very welcome: in fact quite the reverse. The other
foxes were staring at him as if he had LOSER written
all over his face. He wondered if they knew why he
was here. He felt a flicker of his old pride run through
his thin bones. Let them stare if they wanted to: he
didn't care! He glared back at them haughtily.

'The first thing we do at every session is to introduce ourselves to the group and let everyone else know how we're feeling and if we think we're making progress.' Dr Thicket gave Thaddeus a sugary smile. 'It helps to share.'

Thaddeus offered her a weak grin in response. He wasn't really a *sharing* sort of fox. And he didn't want to introduce himself. He was the infamous

Thaddeus E. Fox. Everyone ought to know who he was already!

Dr Thicket hadn't finished. 'When we've done that, we'll split up into teams and do some role-play to improve our confidence.'

'What's that?' Thaddeus asked huffily. Dr Thicket's sugary smile was really beginning to annoy him. It wasn't very *foxy*.

Dr Thicket was undeterred by his tone. 'Well,' she said smoothly, 'one of you might pretend to be a human with a gun, or an angry badger, for example, and the other one has to work out what to do to stop their tail getting blown off or being bashed up or whatever.'

'You mean come up with an evil plan?' Thaddeus said with more enthusiasm. That sounded much more up his street. He was ace at evil plans. Or at least he used to be.

'Well, it doesn't necessarily have to be *evil*,' the fox-iatrist said, her smile wilting a little. 'It could just be about being sensible and not getting hurt.'

Being sensible and not getting hurt? That was one of

the most stupid things Thaddeus E. Fox had ever heard, especially coming from another fox. Foxes were supposed to be superior predators, for goodness' sake, not spineless failures like rabbits. 'But evil plans are always the best ones,' he argued. 'Otherwise you'll never become a great villain, like me.'

'Yes, well . . .' Dr Thicket began, but Thaddeus interrupted.

'What happens when you've worked out a plan?' he demanded rudely.

The fox-iatrist looked as if she was choosing her words carefully. 'You act out the scene together, then you discuss it with the group to see if anyone thinks you should have handled things . . . er . . . *differently*.'

Thaddeus raised his eyebrows. He had absolutely no intention of discussing his evil plans with any of these foxes, let alone taking their advice as to how he should handle things. The sooner they learned who was boss, the better. 'I see,' he said coldly.

'Good, then let's make a start,' said the fox-iatrist, sounding relieved. 'Roger, why don't you begin?'

'Okay.' A small, timid-looking fox stood up. 'My

name is Roger and I'm scared of baked beans,' he said.

Everyone clapped except Thaddeus, who chortled under his breath. *Scared of baked beans?!* What a joke!

Dr Thicket glared at him. 'And why is that, Roger?'

'Because I once knocked over a whole shelf of them in STACK 'EM HIGH SELL 'EM CHEAP SUPERMARKET and was nearly buried alive,' Roger whispered, a tear running down his cheek.

Thaddeus rolled his eyes. 'Roger the Bodger,' he muttered.

The fox-iatrist ignored him. 'And how is your recovery coming on?'

'Quite well,' Roger said. 'I can now look at a picture of beans on toast without crying.'

Big deal! thought Thaddeus.

'Excellent!' said the fox-iatrist. 'We'll have you raiding STACK 'EM HIGH SELL 'EM CHEAP SUPERMARKET again in no time. What about you, Sylvia?'

Everyone turned to look at a stocky silver fox who was lying on the rug beside the door. Thaddeus grimaced. She was missing her tail.

'My name is Sylvia,' she said. 'I used to be a champion dustbin raider, then one morning I got thrown into a bin lorry mid-raid and was trapped in the crusher. I lost my tail. I thought I'd never get my balance back.'

'Ooh,' tutted the group.

'But I'm definitely getting better,' Sylvia reassured them. 'Yesterday I managed to walk along the garden wall without falling off for the first time since the accident.'

'Good for you, Sylvia!' cried Dr Thicket.

Yippee! thought Thaddeus sarcastically.

Round they went in the semicircle. Mostly the foxes had suffered at the hands of humans. One had received a nasty pecking from a murder of crows. Another had been bullied by a bunch of mean badgers.

Every time someone finished speaking, the group clapped their paws together and murmured sympathetically, except Thaddeus, who listened to each story with growing incredulity. It was becoming increasingly obvious to him that this whole weedy, touchy-feely, sharing, role-play, discussion, therapy thing was a load of phony-baloney. What these foxes needed was something different altogether, something much more satisfying.

Yes! thought Thaddeus. *What they needed was REVENGE.*

It was obvious really. He could see it now with complete clarity. It was what *they* needed. And it was what *he* needed, and had done since the day he last suffered defeat at the wings of Professor Rooster and his elite-chicken squad.

REVENGE! REVENGE! REVENGE! The word went round in his head. On the person who stacked the baked beans at STACK 'EM HIGH SELL 'EM CHEAP SUPERMARKET; on the man who operated the rubbish crusher on the bin lorry; on the pesky pecking murder of crows; on those bullying badgers; and above all on flocking, clucking, cheeping, chirping chickens everywhere, especially ones who did kung fu, dropped brick-eggs on your head and got your posh clothes covered in cow's muck . . .

'STOP!' he thundered suddenly.

The room went quiet.

'Can't you see?' shouted Thaddeus. 'All this talking is a waste of time.' He paused dramatically. 'What you need is REVENGE!'

He expected his announcement to be greeted with wild cheers of appreciation. To his surprise, however, the convalescing foxes appeared horrified.

Dr Thicket's eyes narrowed. 'We don't use the R word here,' she hissed. 'It's forbidden.'

'Why?' Thaddeus asked. He had no idea what the problem was, but nevertheless he felt grimly satisfied. At least he'd managed to wipe the sugary smile off the fox-iatrist's chops.

'Because it is not one of our methods,' Dr Thicket snapped back.

'Why not?' Thaddeus retorted.

'The R word only makes things worse!' Roger whimpered, his eyes wide with fear.

'Rubbish!' snarled Thaddeus. 'It's the best word in the world.'

'No, it's not!' Sylvia held her paws over Roger's ears. 'The R word means you just get stuck in the past. You never get to move on with your life.' She

77

gave Thaddeus a look of contempt. 'I knew you were a loser when I heard you were afraid of chickens,' she added.

Thaddeus went red. So they did know! And now they were mocking him. Well, he'd show them! He, Thaddeus E. Fox, would soon be restored to his former glory by the R word, while they slunk about in the shadows, scared to look at a tin of baked beans.

'I am not a loser!' Thaddeus roared. He felt intoxicated with adrenaline. The doctor was right – the sea air had done him a power of good. He was cured! 'I am Thaddeus E. Fox, leader of the MOST WANTED Club of villains. And revenge is my favourite word.' He grinned at Roger. 'Go on, say it. It feels good.'

Roger started to cry.

Dr Thicket stood up. 'If you don't stop right now, Thaddeus, I'm afraid I'll have to ask you to leave,' she threatened.

'Revenge, revenge, revenge, revenge!' Thaddeus sang.

The other foxes blocked their ears.

78

'Okay, you asked for it.' The Fox–iatrist gave a whistle. Two burly security foxes arrived on the scene. They grabbed Thaddeus by the tail and hauled him backwards out of the kitchen to the hall.

'REVENGE, REVENGE, REVENGE!' he screamed as he was dragged towards the front door.

'Good riddance!' A large hind paw connected with Thaddeus's backside. He landed with a bump on the grass. A moment later the attic window opened. Someone threw down his bag. Thaddeus got to his feet with dignity. He didn't mind the cold air, or the darkness, or the fact that he was alone. He still felt heady with excitement. He would show that dopey fox–iatrist whose methods were best! He picked up his bag and trotted towards the gate.

Just then an enormous owl swooped towards him out of the darkness. Thaddeus felt it sink its talons painfully into his coat. Almost before he knew what was happening, he found himself being lifted into the air and borne away across the sea.

Chapter Eight

The next day Amy woke early. A horrible snorting was coming from somewhere nearby. At first she thought the caravan park had been invaded by a herd of pigs. Then she remembered. Granny Wishbone and her beach volleyball pals were sleeping in another caravan a few doors down.

She fluffed out her feathers and stretched. If it weren't for the proximity of Granny Wishbone, and the fact that they were all in mortal danger from an evil, fossil-collecting eagle owl, the caravan would have been a lovely place for a chicken to spend a holiday. Probably, if you were a human, it would have looked just as dilapidated on the inside as it did on the outside but, being a chicken, Amy thought it was ace.

At one end of the caravan there were three snug little bedrooms with two narrow beds in each. The chicks slept in one, the young hens in another and the

old hens in the third. Those who wanted a little more space to stretch out slept on blankets on the floor and those who wanted a bit of privacy roosted in the cupboards. Next to the bedrooms was the toilet area. (This was only to be used if you were desperate in the night, of course, so you didn't make the whole place smelly.) And at the front of the caravan was the sitting room.

The sitting room was where the rest of the hens slept. The room was open plan. At one end a giant corner sofa stretched around three sides of the caravan's interior with views towards the sea. The sofas were old and scruffy, with large quantities of stuffing hanging out of the cushions. In front of the sofas on a rickety table was a small TV, which the chickens had managed to rig up with an aerial so that it picked up the BBC (Bird Broadcasting Corporation). At the other end of the room was the kitchen. It had loads of interesting nooks and crannies full of pots and pans and brushes and buckets and clothes pegs, as well as a small fridge stuffed with bags of mealworm (raided from the park-keeper's van when she wasn't looking) and recycled plastic bottles full of freshly squeezed worm juice. There was even a mini hoover attached to the wall, which the chickens used to keep the place clean.

It was as if the place had been fitted out for fowl.

Amy let out a satisfied cluck. Once the mission was over she was looking forward to putting her feet up. But for now, there was work to be done. Very quietly, so as not to disturb the flock, she woke up Boo and Ruth. The three chickens tiptoed over to the kitchen and made themselves some breakfast. Then they let themselves out of the caravan and went to find James Pond.

The duck agent was pacing up and down outside the bin enclosure, a glazed expression on his face.

'What's wrong with you?' asked Boo.

'I didn't get a wink of sleep,' James Pond snapped.

For once, Amy felt a teeny-weeny bit sorry for the duck. Unfortunately, the caravan that the granny hens had chosen to occupy was right next to his sleeping quarters.

SNORT! SNORE! SNORT! SNORE! SNORT!

83

SNORE! The granny hens were still out for the count. Amy put her hands to her ears. When you got this close they sounded more like a collection of angry warthogs than a mere herd of pigs.

'What about the mission?' Boo said. 'Are we going or what?'

'I can't go like this!' James Pond quacked. 'I feel like a zombie right now. Those grannies spent half the night partying and the rest of it on the loo. I need to catch up with my sleep. I have to be in perfect shape to take on Raptorov.'

'We could do it,' Amy suggested.

'What? After your performance yesterday! Don't make me laugh!' James Pond turned his back on them and waddled off towards the other end of the caravan park.

'Stupid duck!' Amy muttered. She had a good mind to prove him wrong.

'Let it go, Amy,' Boo sighed, reading her thoughts. 'We can't do anything anyway – he's got the homing device. We'll just have to wait until he's in a better mood. Don't you agree, Ruth?'

But Ruth wasn't listening. She was puzzling over something else.

'What is it?' asked Amy.

'I'm just thinking about last night,' Ruth replied.

'What about it?'

'Well, James Pond said the granny chickens went outside the caravan in the night to use the loos . . .'

'So?'

'. . . Raptorov *still* didn't attack them. I mean, why not? They were sitting ducks.'

Boo and Amy thought for a minute.

'Maybe they were too scrawny?' Boo said. 'I mean, you wouldn't get much meat off them. They're all bone and feathers and knobbly knees.'

'I don't think that would normally bother an eagle owl,' Ruth said. 'They eat everything and plop out the bits they can't digest in pellets. No –' she paced up and down – 'Raptorov's biding his time.'

'And you think it's to do with the fossils?' Boo guessed.

'Maybe,' Ruth said. She sighed. 'I wish I'd got a closer look at them yesterday when we were at the

cave. If I knew what type of fossils Raptorov was collecting, I might have a better idea of what he wants to do with them.'

Amy felt guilty. That was her fault for having a rumbly tummy, although unlike James Pond, Ruth was far too nice to say so.

'Why don't we go and have a look on the beach?' she suggested. 'Maybe we'll find something fossily there that will give us a clue.'

'Good idea, Amy,' said Ruth, giving her a pat on the back. 'You know, you're really beginning to think like a scientist.'

'What do you mean?'

'Well, a good scientist always finds a way around a problem to help them solve it. That's what you've just done.'

Amy glowed with pride.

'We'd better go before the grannies wake up and start practising for the volleyball championships,' Boo said.

The three chickens scrambled down the cliff path as fast as they could and began to search amongst the rocks.

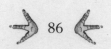

'What exactly are we looking for?' Boo asked, turning over the stones with her strong wings.

'Anything with an unusual pattern,' Ruth replied.

'Like that, you mean?' Amy said, pointing at one Boo had uncovered.

The stone was flat and oval in shape, and about thirty centimetres in length. It contained the impression of something that looked a bit like the last joint of one of Amy's toes, except it was at least a hundred times bigger. 'Do you think it belonged to a giant chicken?' she said in awe.

Ruth's eyes were nearly popping out of her head. 'Not a chicken exactly,' she whispered. 'One of our distant ancestors.'

Distant ancestors? Amy was perplexed.

'Remember what I told you in the science lesson back at Dudley Academy, Amy?' Ruth said.

Suddenly the penny dropped. Amy knew exactly what she meant. She gawped at Ruth.

Boo looked from one to the other. 'Could one of you two please tell me what's going on?'

'Go ahead, Ruth,' Amy said.

'It's the fossil of a dinosaur claw,' Ruth said. 'I think it belonged to a T. rex.'

'A T. rex?! But why would Raptorov want something like that?' Boo scratched her head.

'I don't know,' Ruth said in a worried voice, 'but something tells me, the sooner we fit that homing device on him, the better. I just hope we won't be too late.'

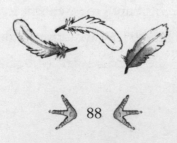

Chapter Nine

Thaddeus E. Fox was having another dream. Only this one wasn't about chickens. It was about owls: one specific owl to be more precise, with enormous talons and a bill that could rip through branches. In his dream it was looming over him, its unblinking eyes centimetres from his face, swaying gently from side to side in time with some dramatic classical music.

Daaaaa – du-du-du-du-du – da-daaaaa – da-daaaaa – du-du-du-du-du – daaaaa.

The music ebbed and flowed like the sea as Thaddeus fought for consciousness. The sea. That was it! Thaddeus remembered now. He was beside the sea. The events of the previous night came flooding back to him. Arriving at the convalescent home . . . the therapy session . . . being thrown out by the security foxes . . . being lifted into the sky by a huge owl. His eyelids flew open in alarm. To his horror, he found that it wasn't a dream after all. The owl was right in front of him, staring at him impassively with its huge orange eyes.

Thaddeus edged backwards. He was in a dark cave with a smooth stone floor.

His heart raced. The owl planned to devour him. That was why it had snatched him from the clifftop and brought him here.

Daaaaa – du-du-du-du-du – da-daaaa – da-daaaa – du-du-du-du-du – daaaaa.

The music was reaching a crescendo. Cymbals banged and crashed. He edged further back, desperately looking for a way to escape. His brush connected with the wall of the cave. He was trapped!

The owl shuffled towards him. 'So,' it said in a thick Russian accent, 'you are Thaddeus E. Fox, the evil villain?'

'Who are you?' Somehow Thaddeus found his voice. 'What do you want with me?'

'I am Vladimir Alexei Raptorov,' came the reply. 'I too am an evil villain. We are like brothers, you and I.' The owl rotated its head in the direction of

the music and listened for a moment, before rotating it back again. 'Tchaikovsky,' he said, 'my favourite composer. I find his work inspiring. This is one of his greatest pieces – *Swan Lake*. It is a ballet. Do you know the story?'

Thaddeus shook his head.

'It is the tale of an evil sorcerer who turns a princess and her friends into beautiful swans,' Raptorov said. 'In the end the sorcerer's spell is broken by the death of the princess and her true love. The rest of the swans return to human form and the sorcerer and his daughter must live as birds forever as punishment for their crime.' The owl gave a series of clicks with its bill that might have passed for an ironic laugh. 'Tchaikovsky's only failing was that he was a human, and not a bird, otherwise the story would have had a much better ending: they would *all* have lived as birds forever! Do you not agree, Mr Fox?'

Thaddeus swallowed. Raptorov was clearly insane. He decided to try and humour him. 'Er, yes,' he said. 'Absolutely. *Swan Lake*. Lovely tune, rubbish ending – I've always thought that.'

He was rewarded by a nod of the owl's head. 'I see that you are a villain of taste, Mr Fox,' Raptorov said. 'I think we have much in common.'

'We do?' Thaddeus wondered what he could possibly have in common with a mad, cave-dwelling, Tchaikovsky-obsessed eagle owl.

'Oh yes.' The owl inclined its head to one side and gave him a quizzical look. 'I was outside the farmhouse, listening to your conversation with the other foxes . . .' it said softly.

'Ah,' said Thaddeus, embarrassed, 'about that chicken thing . . .'

The owl stared him down. 'I do not need to know the details. The point is you are quite right, Mr Fox. Revenge is what we evil villains feed off. It is our life-blood. It is what makes us tick. You seek revenge on chickens. And I seek revenge on humans. That is why I brought you here. I think we may be of use to one another.'

'You mean you're not going to eat me?'

'*Probably* not,' said Raptorov, lingering a little too long on the word 'probably' for Thaddeus's liking.

'I wish us to be friends. Come, let me show you something.' The owl shuffled off towards the other end of the cave. Thaddeus followed him. The owl led him through a tunnel in the rock face into another cave. Thaddeus looked about him in bewilderment. The edge of the cave was lined on two sides with a low rock shelf. Arrayed upon one shelf was a collection of stones. Standing upon the other was a rack of test tubes, several hypodermic syringes and various tiny bottles of liquid.

'This is my laboratory,' Raptorov said. 'This is where I shall conduct my experiments.'

Thaddeus gulped. This was getting creepier and creepier, like something out of a horror film. 'Experiments?' he echoed.

The owl appeared not to have heard him. Instead it said, 'Have you ever thought what the world would be like, Mr Fox, if there were no humans?'

Thaddeus was having trouble keeping up. The owl talked in riddles. 'Er, yes, and, er, no,' he replied cautiously.

'Well, I have,' said Raptorov. 'You see, Mr Fox, I was once imprisoned by humans. They used me for

their own experiments.'

'What sort of experiments?'

'Genetic engineering,' said Raptorov. 'They gave me the DNA of other species to improve my already formidable talents. They made me the most superior bird in the whole world. Little did they know that their efforts would be rewarded by the annihilation of their own species.'

'Ah, so that's what you're after, a spot of annihilation,' said Thaddeus. He could see that Raptorov was warming up to a big-head villain speech. Usually it was him who made those, but he had the feeling it wouldn't be wise to interrupt the owl at this particular moment. His shoulders were still painful from where Raptorov's talons had pierced his coat. He didn't want any more perforations in his fur.

'Freedom to an owl is everything.' Raptorov spoke in a chilling voice. 'And the humans took away my freedom, Mr Fox, for ten long years. That is why I hate humans, just like you hate chickens. That is why I want what you want: REVENGE!' He chuckled softly.

'Yes, good idea, so what's the evil plan?' Thaddeus

said, hoping to cut the speech short.

He didn't succeed. Like all evil villains, Raptorov enjoyed an audience. 'It is this, Mr Fox: to create a world where the natural order is restored; where birds rule the planet and humans are extinct. A world very much like it was millions of years ago, during the time of the dinosaurs . . .'

He's barking! thought Thaddeus, although he nodded in what he hoped was an evil, villainous sort of way.

'Did you know, Mr Fox, that birds are the last living dinosaurs?' Raptorov said.

'Er, no,' Thaddeus replied. He didn't usually pay much attention to birds, except to eat them.

'It is the truth, Mr Fox. We are. But instead of being what we once were, we have evolved to become weak. When I was in captivity, however, I began to see a way to make our species strong again. What if more of us could be genetically modified, like me? What if we could become like the dinosaur birds of old?' He paused. 'I am a patient bird, Mr Fox. I could have escaped my captors sooner but instead I waited. I learned everything I could about genetic engineering; about how to make a rat fly and a sloth run as fast as a cheetah . . .'

Completely bonkers! Thaddeus nodded vigorously.

'. . . Eventually I was ready. I made my escape. All I had to do was find a place where dinosaurs had once roamed. That is why I chose Stormy Island: the cliffs here are rich in dinosaur fossils . . .' He gestured at his collection of rocks.

Stormy Island? The tombstone-shaped rock he'd spotted from his room at the convalescent home for distressed foxes? So that's where he was! Thaddeus had been wondering. He felt as if it was time he said something intelligent. Raptorov seemed to be expecting it. 'So, what exactly are the . . . er . . . fossils for?' he said. Personally he couldn't see how a bunch of old dinosaur rocks could make birds rule the world or humans extinct. The only thing they might come in useful for was to bash Raptorov over the head with while he was in mid-rant so that Thaddeus could make his escape.

Raptorov fixed him with his beady eyes. 'I have discovered a way to extract DNA from them,' he pronounced. 'I will use it to modify the DNA of bird-kind to create a race of pre-historic dino-birds.

Imagine, Mr Fox, if you will, the power of such a race. Very soon we would rule the world and the humans would become extinct.'

Dino-birds? Even if Raptorov was crackers (which he obviously was), Thaddeus had to admit it was a brilliantly evil plan. Ambitious too. He had to admire the owl's audacity. He, Thaddeus, tended to think in less global terms, although he had once set up a foxy battery farm in the city. And it would have worked, if it hadn't been for Rooster and his elite-chicken squad. Thaddeus ground his teeth. The thought made him seethe.

'I see you are thinking of your own problem, Mr Fox,' the owl said, regarding him steadily, 'and wishing you could come up with an equally evil plan to annihilate chickens.'

'I'm just a bit rusty, that's all,' Thaddeus said huffily.

'Indeed,' Raptorov inclined his head. 'I meant no offence. I wish to help you, if you are prepared to help me.'

'How?'

'I need birds to conduct my experiments on,' said

Raptorov. 'Your job, my friend, is to lure them here, without them suspecting anything. If you do this successfully, I will allow you to test out my new breed of dino-birds on your chicken enemies. I promise you, no chicken will ever challenge you again. Your revenge will be complete.'

'What if I refuse?' asked Thaddeus.

'Then I will kill you.'

Thaddeus sighed. It was a bit of a no-brainer, really. He didn't fancy his chances against Raptorov, not in his current emaciated state, and even if he could overpower the owl, he didn't know how to escape from the caves or get away from the island. 'Very well,' he said. 'I'll do it. Do you have any particular birds in mind?'

'Yes,' Raptorov said smugly. 'They are birds of the most horrible kind I have ever seen: scrawny, mean and utterly revolting in their habits. Combined with the correct dinosaur DNA they will be invincible.'

'Where do I find them?' asked Thaddeus.

'At Stormy Cliff Caravan Park,' said Raptorov. 'They are taking part in the annual Granny Hen

Beach Volleyball Championships. There is no time to waste, Mr Fox. You must lure them here across the causeway tonight so that I may begin my work.'

A causeway? That made things easier. A sly grin spread over Thaddeus's face. 'Do you have a pen and paper by any chance?' he said.

Chapter Ten

The next day Amy woke up to the sound of furious quacking. James Pond was outside, and unlike the previous morning it sounded as if he was raring to go!

'Pssst!' she prodded Boo and Ruth. 'It's James Pond. It's time for the mission.'

The three chickens let themselves out of the caravan quietly.

'There you are!' James Pond snapped. 'About time! We've got a new problem. The granny hens have vanished.'

'Raptorov!' gasped Amy. The eagle owl had struck at last.

'Not just Raptorov,' said James Pond shortly.

'What do you mean, not just Raptorov?' asked Boo.

'Take a look at this.' James Pond thrust a piece of paper towards them.

You are invited to an all night
~~experiment~~ {rave!}

Games and Prizes!

Free limpets — all you can eat!

Sick buckets provided!

Knobbly knee competition!

Ugliest granny hen contest!

Boniest wing championship!

Cave volleyball!

Pin the tail on the ~~dinosaur~~ donkey!

Raptorov's Laboratory Disco
The Caves
Stormy Island
Near Stormy Cliff

Directions: take the causeway. Passable until 9pm.

'Thaddeus E. Fox!' exclaimed Amy. The invitation had all the hallmarks of the fox's work. He was notorious for inviting trusting chickens to pretend parties and then trying to eat them. 'What's *he* doing here?'

'Search me,' said James Pond, 'but it looks like he's teamed up with Raptorov. We'll have to surprise them both. Hopefully they'll be fast asleep, full of chicken.'

'You think they've eaten all the granny hens?' Boo asked with a shudder.

'Of course,' said James Pond. 'What else would they do with them?'

It was a good question. Amy had started to believe that maybe Raptorov wasn't interested in chickens after all and that Ruth was right; he was here for the fossils. But teaming up with Thaddeus E. Fox and attacking the granny hens put paid to that theory.

'We don't have any weapons to defeat Thaddeus,' she said.

'Then we'll just have to set up a decoy,' James Pond

replied. 'You three distract Thaddeus while I fit the homing device on Raptorov. Once Thaddeus sees what we've done to his new owl buddy my guess is he won't hang around. Especially without the MOST WANTED Club to back him up. Now come on.' He began to limber up ready for take-off.

'Should we take the Emergency Chicken Pack?' asked Amy.

'I think we'd better,' said Ruth. She strapped the bulky backpack on over her flight booster engine, her face pensive.

'Don't worry, Ruth,' said Amy, 'we can manage Thaddeus.'

'It's not that,' Ruth said.

'What is it then?'

'I've just got a feeling something's wrong. The invitation said something about Raptorov's "laboratory" and "experiments" and "dinosaurs" before Thaddeus crossed it out. What if Raptorov *hasn't* eaten the granny hens at all? What if he's using them for something else?'

Amy and Boo glanced at one another. Ruth was

still sticking to her alternative fossil theory, despite the evidence.

'Like what though?' asked Boo.

'That's the trouble,' Ruth sighed. 'I still don't know.'

'Hurry up!' James Pond quacked impatiently from above.

'We're coming!' shouted the chickens and off they went towards the island.

This time they landed on the ledge outside the cave. There was no sign of the granny hens or the villains.

Ruth took out the evil baddie Geiger counter and held it towards the cave entrance. The needle shot to the top of the dial. *Raptorov and Thaddeus!* The baddies' combined evilness was too much for the Geiger counter. The two of them together were literally off the scale.

James Pond took the lead. He crept into the cave, the chickens following behind.

They were wearing their infra-red super-spec headsets so that they could see in the darkness. Ruth paused at the pile of stones. She picked one up and inspected it carefully. Her face assumed an even more worried expression. Silently she offered the stone to Boo and Amy to take a look.

Amy could see the outline of another claw. This one was smaller than the one they had found on the beach, but it was still unmistakably that of a dinosaur.

Suddenly Ruth let out a gasp. Amy looked at her in surprise. They mustn't make any noise or they might wake up Raptorov. Everyone knew that. She

frowned. It wasn't like Ruth to make silly mistakes. That was normally what *she* did!

James Pond gave Ruth a furious look and waddled on towards the back of the cave. Amy was about to follow with Boo, but Ruth blocked their way. She pointed to the fossils, then reached inside the Emergency Chicken Pack and pulled something out. Amy blinked. It wasn't one of Professor Rooster's surprise gadgets: it was the book about bird evolution. Ruth leafed through it frantically until she found the page she wanted and held the book up for the others to look at. The picture was of a flying dinosaur with keen eyes, a huge bill, bony wings and razor-sharp teeth.

Amy peered at it, trying to puzzle out what Ruth was telling them. The dinosaur bird looked remarkably like one of the granny hens: mean and scrawny and sly, except that the granny hens had false teeth and couldn't fly. Unless they had a shot of dinosaur DNA, of course . . .

Suddenly Amy had one of her occasional flashes of chicken genius. She knew exactly what Ruth

was trying to tell them. Raptorov hadn't eaten the grannies. He wanted to turn them into terrifying dino-birds, like the ones in the picture, using the fossils he'd collected. They had to get out of there fast! *But first she had to warn James Pond!*

Amy scuttled to the back of the cave in search of him. But the duck had disappeared. He must have gone into the tunnel! Just then she heard a horrible noise coming from behind the wall of rock, followed by a frantic quacking.

James Pond! Whatever it was that Raptorov had created, it had caught the duck agent. Swallowing her fear, Amy crept into the tunnel. She took a few steps and stopped. The holster containing the homing device lay on the ground next to a few feathers, but there was no sign of James Pond.

'SQUAWWWKKKKKKKK-KA-KA-KA-KA!'

Amy froze. The creature was still in the tunnel somewhere up ahead. It must have heard her.

SCRATCH! SCRATCH! SCRATCH! The sound of claws scraping on rock heralded the creature's approach. *It was coming towards her!*

 108

Amy grabbed the holster and slung it over her shoulder. Then she shot back along the tunnel and across the cave as fast as her legs would carry her.

The noise was getting louder. Amy glanced back. A shadow loomed against the wall. It was even more terrifying than the hunched shadow of Raptorov. She could see the outline of a hideous, hopping, bunched-up bird, like a pelican, only scrawnier, with bony wings and an enormous beak full of razor-sharp teeth. It appeared to be leaning on a zimmer frame.

'SQUAWWWKKKKKKKK-KA-KA-KA-KA!'

Amy had reached the ledge. Boo and Ruth were waiting, just in case she needed help. But this time all three chickens managed their controls without problem. *ZOOM!* Up flew the warriors into the air.

Amy looked down. Once again the ledge was empty. The creature had gone back inside the tunnel. But they had been too late to save James Pond.

Chapter Eleven

'So now what do we do?' Amy, Boo and Ruth were holding an emergency meeting underneath the caravan where they couldn't be overheard. The rest of the chickens had been rounded up by Boo and told to stay inside and not accept ANY invitations to parties, however tempting they might seem. Boo had also told them that Raptorov and Thaddeus E. Fox had tricked the granny hens into visiting Stormy Island, but not about the owl's evil plan to turn the grannies into dino-birds. There was no point in spreading panic amongst the flock.

'Maybe the dinosaur DNA will wear off,' Boo said hopefully. 'Then we can go and fetch the grannies back, rescue James Pond and send the villains packing, like we planned.'

'Maybe,' said Ruth. She shook her head ruefully. 'I should have seen this coming.'

'It's not your fault, Ruth!' Amy said stoutly.

'I should have realised though,' Ruth insisted. 'Remember what you said when Professor Rooster first told us about Raptorov, Amy?'

'No,' said Amy. She didn't have a very large brain capacity for remembering things.

'Well, I was telling you what genetic engineering is, and you said, "if chickens wanted to be really fierce, you could give them the DNA of a T. rex".'

'Oh yes.' Amy remembered now. She frowned. 'But I swear you said that was impossible?'

'I thought it was,' said Ruth, 'because dinosaurs died out sixty million years ago and I thought you couldn't extract their DNA. But obviously I was wrong. Raptorov must have found a way of extracting dinosaur DNA from fossils. That's why he's been collecting them. I don't know how I could have been so blind!'

'But why does he even want to make dino-birds?' Amy said.

Ruth shrugged. 'Power, I suppose. That's what makes most villains tick, apart from revenge. Think about it: with an army of granny raptors at his back,

Raptorov will be the most powerful bird in the world. Now tell us again, Amy. What exactly did you see when you went after James Pond?'

Amy described the hideous shadow of the dino-bird.

'Hmm,' said Ruth, 'that's bad, very bad. It sounds like he's given the grannies a shot of raptor DNA.'

'Is a raptor a type of dinosaur?' asked Boo.

Ruth nodded. 'Yes, one of the most ferocious types that ever lived.'

'More ferocious than a T. rex?' asked Amy.

'Possibly,' said Ruth. 'Raptors were smaller but they hunted in packs. They were more intelligent too.'

Amy shivered. The idea of the granny dino-birds hunting in a pack was horrible. The grannies were bad enough when they were just playing beach volleyball and stamping on other chickens' sandcastles. 'Why didn't it come after us when we took off?' she wondered.

'My guess is the granny raptors' wings aren't strong enough,' Ruth said. 'I mean, chickens can't fly

much anyway, especially if they're old: adding raptor juice isn't going to change that. If Raptorov wants his dino-birds to fly, he's either going to have to choose different birds to experiment on or find a fossil of a pterodactyl and give some of that to the grannies. A pterodactyl is one of the flying dinosaurs I showed you in the book, by the way.'

Yikes, thought Amy, remembering how fearsome they looked.

'If he does that, he'll spread terror across the sky,' Ruth said. 'No animal will be safe: not even humans. And no chickens either. We'll get minced.'

'We have to stop him!' Amy cried.

'I agree,' said Ruth. 'The question is how.'

'At least we've got the homing device,' Boo said.

'We don't have the laser torch though,' Amy pointed out.

'Maybe there's something in the Emergency Chicken Pack that we can use,' Boo suggested. 'The professor always gives us some good gadgets.'

'Let's have a look.' Ruth untied the string of the backpack and shook the contents out onto the ground.

Owl cave sat-nav

Full body armour and helmet

CD of *Silly Billy's Favourite Chicken Party Songs*

Ballet outfit

'*Silly Billy's Favourite Chicken Party Songs.*' Amy grabbed the CD. 'I love that!' It had all the tunes she had enjoyed singing along to with her friends at Perrin's Farm, like 'Do the Funky Chicken', 'Old MacDonald Had a Farm' and the 'Hokey Kokey'.

'What's it for though?' Boo wondered.

'Hmmm.' Ruth was going through the items individually. 'Well, the owl cave sat-nav is for us to find our way around the cave system, and we can use the body armour to help us fit the homing device . . .

'What about this?' Amy held up the ballet outfit.

Ruth looked at it thoughtfully. 'Maybe it has something to do with Raptorov's passion for the composer, Tchaikovsky? He wrote lots of ballet music.' She shrugged. 'We'll work it out when the time comes.'

Maybe, thought Amy. The chickens usually managed to find a use for most of the contents of the Emergency Chicken Pack when they got into dangerous situations. The problem was, this time Professor Rooster had only packed things to defeat Raptorov: he wasn't expecting Thaddeus E. Fox or

a pack of genetically modified raptor hens to show up as well. This was turning out to be their toughest chicken mission yet.

'Are you sure there's nothing else?' she asked.

Ruth gave the Emergency Chicken Pack a shake. A small round plastic box fell out. She picked it up and twisted the lid off carefully. Inside were three sets of tiny headphones. 'Wow!' said Ruth.

'What are they?' asked Boo.

'They're silent communication devices,' Ruth replied. 'They allow us to talk to one another just by picking up our brainwaves so Raptorov won't hear us.'

'You mean like a sort of walkie-thinkie?' said Amy, who used to watch action movies with her dad when she lived at Perrin's Farm.

Ruth grinned at her. 'Exactly. You're getting really good at this science stuff, Amy.'

'Okay, so when do we make our move?' asked Boo.

'It's too late to do anything else this afternoon,' Ruth said. The day had slipped away. It was already

late afternoon and it wouldn't be long before the nocturnal eagle owl would be awake again. 'I don't like it much but we'll have to wait until first light. Meanwhile we need to protect the flock.'

Boo and Amy nodded grimly. Another night in the caravan was another night of danger for the chickens of Stormy Cliff, especially with an army of granny raptors hiding a short distance away in the caves of Stormy Island. It would be easy for them to cross the causeway again at low tide under Raptorov's command.

'We should board up the windows and the door of the caravan,' Amy said. 'You know what the grannies are like with those zimmer frames!' The chickens had once been attacked by the grannies at a place called Fogsham Farm. The experience had been terrifying. And that was when the grannies were normal hens!

'Let's see if we can find something to use in the park keeper's shed,' Boo said.

The chickens emerged from under the caravan and scuttled over to the shed. They pushed open the door.

'Bingo!' said Boo.

Besides the lawnmower and some rusty gardening equipment, a quantity of old fence posts stood stacked in one corner.

Amy hopped up onto the shelf. 'There's a hammer and nails up here,' she said.

'Chuck the hammer down,' said Boo.

'Okay, watch out!' Amy heaved the hammer off the shelf. It landed with a crash on the floor. The

nails were lighter. She could just about manage those. Cradling the box in her wings, she dropped off the shelf after the hammer.

'I'll get the others to help,' Ruth said.

Very soon she had organised the flock into teams of helpers. Between them the chickens carried the fence posts, the hammer and the box of nails back to the caravan.

'What's this all about?' asked one of the mother hens anxiously.

'It's just a precaution,' Boo said calmly. 'Don't worry.'

'Don't you think we should tell them about the granny raptors?' Amy whispered. 'Just in case?'

'We'll tell them once the barricades are up,' Boo whispered back. 'They'll feel safer then.'

'Okay.'

The chickens set to work, hammering the wooden posts over the insides of the window frames and the door. At last the job was completed.

Amy banged in the last nail and stood back and surveyed their work. She glanced at Boo and Ruth.

They nodded. It was time to tell the flock about Raptorov's experiments.

'Okay,' said Boo, 'everyone grab a worm juice and a few grubs and come and sit down. We've got some bad news.'

Chapter Twelve

Deep within the system of caves inside Stormy Island, the two villains were enjoying a candlelit supper of rabbit stew and mouse dumplings to the tune of Tchaikovsky's Third Piano Concerto. Thaddeus was impressed. Not just by the evilness of the eagle owl or the quality of his undeniably tasty stew or even the stirring music, but by the whole set-up. Raptorov was a villain who knew how to look after himself. He had kitted out the caves perfectly to suit his lifestyle.

Thaddeus had been provided with his own bed cave during his stay, thoughtfully lined with piles of skins to keep out the cold. Then there was the dining cave where they were now – tastefully fitted with a long stone table, soft-mood lighting and a large fireplace for cooking. Next to the dining cave was the larder, replete with as many dead hares and rabbits and pigeons and mice as a fox could want, all hanging by their necks in neat rows from stalactites

in the ceiling on lengths of string. Finally there was a comfy chill-out cave, furnished with fur rugs and sacks full of feathers. (Raptorov had explained to him that normally owls ingested the fur and feathers of their prey and plopped them out in pellets, but he preferred his meat skinned from his time in captivity so why waste the other bits?)

These were the living quarters, and very comfy they were too. At the business end of things – separated from the living quarters by one of the many

tunnels that riddled the island – was the laboratory where Raptorov conducted his experiments. Next to that was a prison cave for his genetically modified dino-birds, where they could be kept for observation and further experimentation if necessary. The prison cave had been chosen for its extra-thick walls, which protected the owl's super-sensitive hearing from the *SQUAWWWKKKKKKKK-KA-KA-KA-KA* of the ghastly raptor grannies so that he could continue his work to the music of *Swan Lake* undisturbed.

There was no doubt in Thaddeus's mind: Raptorov had made a brilliant lair for himself. He thought of his own accommodation back at the burrow in the Deep Dark Woods. He could see now that he had let things go a bit. When he got back he would have a spring clean and invite the former members of the MOST WANTED Club around for dinner. He might even dig an extension. He could do with a super-size larder to store all the chickens he was going to catch with the pack of granny raptors that Raptorov had placed at his disposal! His face took on a lopsided leer. He felt quite restored to the Thaddeus of old. Professor Rooster and his elite-chicken squad had better watch out.

'I see, my friend, that you are beginning to enjoy yourself. Tell me, what are you thinking?' Raptorov said.

Thaddeus told him. He no longer minded talking about Professor Rooster and his team or what he planned to do to them in revenge. It was good therapy.

The owl listened without interruption. 'Ah,' he said, when Thaddeus had finished. 'Now I fully understand *why* you want revenge on chicken-kind.' He twisted his head round slowly one way then the other – a habit he had adopted when he was deep in thought. 'Tell me, my friend, did the three chickens you describe always work alone?'

'Not always,' Thaddeus replied. 'The professor sometimes employed a duck agent as well. His name was Pond, James Pond.'

'Did this duck carry gadgets, by any chance?' Raptorov inquired.

'Yes, he did,' replied Thaddeus. 'Why?'

'Because this morning at first light one of the

granny dino-birds managed to break out of the prison cave. She almost escaped. Fortunately I heard a commotion near the entrance of the caves and was able to stop her by tempting her back with a genetically modified worm. Not, however, before she had attacked an intruder – a large mallard duck wearing a bow tie. It was equipped with a laser torch.'

'That sounds like Pond, all right,' Thaddeus exclaimed.

'Hmmm,' said Raptorov. 'Then it is likely, my friend, that your chicken enemies are not far away. This Professor Rooster must have got wind of my arrival and sent them and the duck to protect the flock at Stormy Cliff.'

'Barn it, I'll bet you're right!' Thaddeus swore softly. 'Rooster has spies everywhere. They must have seen you and reported back to him.'

'It is of no matter.' Raptorov gave a soft chuckle. 'Rooster probably thinks I am here to eat chickens. Little does he know my real plan for world domination!'

'So what shall we do?' asked Thaddeus.

 125

'Do? Twit twoo! It is obvious what we shall do. The granny dino-birds will attack the caravan park tonight. They will bring the flock here to Stormy Island ready for our feast. Then, when Professor Rooster's elite-chicken squad try to rescue them, we shall be waiting.'

'Bravo!' cried Thaddeus, inwardly rejoicing. The three chickens wouldn't have a prayer against Raptorov and the grannies. They were as dead as dodos! 'What about Pond?'

'Well,' said Raptorov, 'I was planning to kill him and hang him in my larder, but I think perhaps there may be another use for him . . .'

'Like what?' Thaddeus asked.

Raptorov's face assumed a smug expression. 'Have you ever heard of a pterodactyl?'

Thaddeus shook his head.

'A pterodactyl was a winged lizard,' Raptorov informed him. 'It had a wingspan of up to twelve metres, excellent eyesight like my own and a mouthful of razor-sharp teeth. It lived approximately one hundred and forty five million years ago. Yesterday

I extracted a small amount of its DNA from a fossil I found here in the caves.' The owl skewered a mouse dumpling and nibbled the meat off delicately. 'I had intended to give it to the granny raptors to make them fly. However, I think I may have found a different use for it.' He gave Thaddeus an owlish wink.

'You mean you're going to make James Pond into a ptero-duck-tyl!' Thaddeus's eyes gleamed in delight.

'Indeed, my friend! And I shall add in a little bit of raptor juice just for fun.' Raptorov clicked his beak in amusement. 'Professor Rooster's elite-chicken squad will never reach Stormy Island; our new ptero-duck-tyl will see to that. Now, to work! You fetch the duck while I prepare the DNA.'

'With pleasure!' Thaddeus snarled.

And with that, the two villains made their way out of the dining cave and along the tunnel to Raptorov's laboratory.

Chapter Thirteen

BASH! BANG! BASH!

Amy had fallen into a fitful sleep. She woke with a start.

BASH! BANG! BASH!

The granny-raptor attack! It had begun.

'Battle stations, everyone!' Ruth cried.

The chickens had worked out a plan before they went to bed. If the granny raptors managed to breach their defences, the weaker members of the flock were to fall back to the bedroom cupboards and shut themselves in, leaving the stronger hens in the kitchen to bombard the genetically modified grannies with all the crockery they could lay their wings on. Meanwhile Amy, Boo and Ruth would blast the attackers with the mite blaster and try to repel the beastly dino-birds that way.

'Quick!'

The able hens hurried to the kitchen, while the

less able hopped out of their beds and made for the relative safety of the cupboards.

Ruth had already fitted a new mite tube into the mite blaster. Boo clutched the gadget in her strong wings. The three chickens hid under the sofa. They were ready for action.

BASH! BANG! BASH!

'SQUAWWWKKKKKKKK-KA-KA-KA-KA!'

Zimmer frames crashed against the doors and windows. Above the din came the horrible rasping rattle of a dozen mean granny raptors on the hunt. For the poor chickens trapped inside the caravan, the experience was truly terrifying.

BASH! BANG! BASH!

'SQUAWWWKKKKKKKK-KA-KA-KA-KA!'

The sound intensified as the frenzied granny raptors pounded at the doors and windows with their metal walking frames. The glass panes smashed in an instant, but so far the wooden barriers were holding. They couldn't get in!

All of a sudden one voice rose above the others.

'SQUAWWWKKKKKKKK-KA-KA-KA-KA!'

Granny Wishbone!' whispered Amy. She'd know that screech anywhere, even if its owner was now a granny raptor–wrestler.

Suddenly there was silence. The attack had stopped: for the time being anyway. But the granny raptors hadn't gone away. The chickens could hear them shuffling about outside the caravan, rattling to themselves. The chickens shifted restlessly, wondering what was happening.

'Nobody move!' Boo ordered. 'We've got to stick to the plan.'

'Ka-ka-ka-ka-ka-ka!' It was Granny Wishbone again. This time her voice had dropped to a squeaky staccato clack, like an ancient lawnmower engine that needed oil. She seemed to be issuing instructions to the other members of the pack.

'Ka-ka-ka-ka-ka-ka!' the granny raptors clacked back.

There was another short silence followed by grunting, a few soft thwacks, accompanying raptor-swearing and a dull thud as something heavy landed awkwardly on the roof.

EEEEEEEEEKKKKKKKKKKKKKKKKKKK!

This noise was even worse. It was a truly horrible sound – like forks scraping across a plate or toenails along a blackboard. The chickens in the caravan began to cluck with fear.

Amy peeped out from under the sofa.

'What is it?' Ruth asked, covering her ears. 'What's making that dreadful noise?'

Amy looked up. To her horror she saw a raptor claw slice through the thin ceiling of the caravan. 'There's one on the roof! It's cutting a hole in the ceiling!' she cried.

At that point all the chickens panicked. Even the most stalwart flocked towards the bedroom cupboards leaving the kitchen unguarded. There was an unseemly struggle as the chickens of Stormy Cliff Caravan Park fought their way into the cupboards. It was every chicken for itself.

'I guess it's up to us now,' Boo said. 'Come on, we'll be safer behind the kitchen units. I'll operate the mite blaster. You two chuck the crockery.'

The three chickens scuttled the short distance to

the kitchenette. Just in time!

EEEEEEEEEKKKKKKKKKKKKKKKKKK!
The granny raptor had almost carved out a circle in the ceiling. THUD! The roof gave way. *CRASH!* The creature dropped like a stone into the living area of the caravan.

'SQUAWWWKKKKKKKK-KA-KA-KA-KA!'

'Jeepers!' said Ruth, staring incredulously at the hideous dino-bird from behind her spectacles.

The granny raptor was a revolting sight. Its shadow had been bad enough, but in the flesh the creature was repulsive. The dino-bird had scaly skin partially covered with feathers, like a half-plucked lizard-chicken. Its hind legs were wrinkled and saggy, like a pair of old stockings, its feet bony and warty, ending in a set of wicked raptor claws. Its upper body wasn't much better. Thin, short wings grasped the zimmer frame, which was the only thing keeping it upright on account of its enormous pelican bill and rows of sharp teeth. With an effort, the dino-bird jerked its head up and removed its teeth. Slavers of sticky drool dropped onto the floor in puddles.

'It's definitely Granny Wishbone,' Amy whispered.

'Amazing!' Ruth whispered back. 'Even her false teeth have been genetically modified!'

Amazing or not, there was no time to dwell on scientific details, for at that moment the granny raptor let out a blood-curdling cry.

'SQUAWWWKKKKKKKK-KA-KA-KA-KA!'

It was the signal the other grannies had been waiting for. One by one they dropped through the caravan roof until there was no space for any more inside.

Granny Wishbone took a deep sniff, and pointed her zimmer frame towards the bedrooms. 'KA-KA-KA-KA-KA-KA!' she shrieked.

Two of the granny raptors advanced in the direction of the flock's hiding place, while the others set about tearing down the barricades to the door and windows with their claws.

'Start the bombardment,' Boo ordered.

From their position behind the kitchen cabinets Amy and Ruth let fly with all the crockery at their disposal.

CRASH! CRASH! CRASH! Cups, saucers, plates and bowls flew at the granny raptors but sharp shards of pottery had no effect on the dino-birds. They bounced off their scaly lizard-skin without harm.

'My turn,' said Boo. She somersaulted onto one of the kitchen cabinets and pulled the trigger on the mite blaster. *WHOOSH!* An infestation of itchy parasites swarmed at the granny raptors. But it was no use. The mites had no effect on the dino-birds' Teflon-coated skin either. They just slid off.

Boo somersaulted back to the others. 'It's not

135

working!' she hissed. 'Now what?''

The activities of the elite-chicken squad had caught the attention of Granny Wishbone. 'KA-KA-KA-KA-KA-KA!' she called softly.

The other dino-birds halted. They turned their crafty eyes on the kitchen.

'Quick, into the saucepan!' Ruth ordered. A large metal pan stood on the bottom shelf of one of the units. The chickens hopped in. Ruth pulled the glass lid over them as quietly as she could. Fortunately it had holes in it to let steam out, so the chickens could breathe.

'KA-KA-KA-KA-KA-KA!' Granny Wishbone had reached the kitchenette. She was looking about with her beady reptile eyes.

'Whatever you do, don't move,' Ruth hissed. 'They can't see you if you don't move.'

The chickens stood stock-still.

SNIFF! SNIFF! SNIFF! 'KA-KA-KA-KA-KA-KA!' Granny Wishbone had picked up the scent of the chicken flock. She veered away from the kitchen towards the bedrooms. The other granny raptors followed.

There was the sound of cupboard doors being wrenched off their hinges and a terrible clucking and squawking. Then, before Boo, Ruth and Amy had time to think what to do, the granny raptors herded the flock out through the door of the caravan and away into the night.

Chapter Fourteen

It didn't take the three plucky members of the elite-chicken squad long to strap on their flight booster engines, pick up the Emergency Chicken Pack and set off in pursuit of the chicken-nappers. One thing Boo, Ruth and Amy could do that the granny raptors couldn't was fly. They hovered high in the sky unseen above the procession of terrified chickens as the bedraggled flock picked its way across the slippery causeway towards Stormy Island, forced on by the mean dino-birds.

Fortunately the sea was calm so there was no danger of the chickens being swept away by the waves, but that was about the only consolation. Raptorov and Thaddeus had timed the attack to perfection. The tide was on the turn. Soon it would start coming in fast, covering the causeway. Once they got to the island, there would be no escape for the chickens of Stormy Cliff Caravan Park until the next low tide.

The three warriors had one more chance to defeat the villains or the flock would perish at the paws of Thaddeus or be turned into dino-birds by Raptorov.

Eventually the sorry procession reached the end of the causeway. The chickens slipped and slithered their way over the rocks to the entrance of the cave and disappeared inside.

'SQUAWWWKKKKKKKK-KA-KA-KA-KA!'

Granny Wishbone let out a triumphant cry and ushered the granny raptors into the cave after their captives.

'We'd better wait until we're sure they've gone,' Ruth said, changing her flight booster engine setting to HELICOPTER mode.

The three chickens hovered in the air some distance above the ledge where the entrance to the caves lay. On closer inspection Stormy Island had lots of ledges and nooks and crannies. Its cratered surface resembled the moon: from far away it looked smooth and pale but when you got close it was pitted and dark.

From somewhere up above they heard the mournful cry of a single seabird.

139

'QUAAAARRRRRK! QUAAAARRRRRK!'

The dismal sound only served to remind them what a desolate place Stormy Island was.

'I wonder what Raptorov feeds the granny raptors on,' Amy said, trying to make conversation while they hovered.

'Well, at least it's not chicken,' Boo said in an attempt at cheerfulness.

'Maybe it's genetically modified worms,' Ruth suggested.

'Yeah, modified with rotten eggs, probably,' Amy joked. It fell a bit flat. None of them was in the mood for laughter.

'QUAAAARRRRRK! QUAAAARRRRRK!'

The cry came again. The chickens looked up. The sound was coming from one of the rocky crags at the top of Stormy Island, but there was no sign of the bird.

Suddenly Amy had an idea. 'Why don't we ask if it will take a message to Professor Rooster and get him to send reinforcements?' she said.

'Because we don't know where Professor Rooster lives,' Boo reminded her.

 140

'But it might be one of his bird spies,' Amy argued. 'In which case it will know where to go.'

'QUAAAARRRRRK! QUAAAARRRRRK!' cried the bird.

'I'm not sure . . .' Ruth began, but Boo interrupted.

'I think it's worth a try,' she said. 'I mean, we're really struggling here. There's only so much we can do with *Silly Billy's Favourite Chicken Party Songs* and a ballet outfit. We need some help.'

'Okay,' Ruth agreed.

The three chickens flew towards the rock face, looking for the bird.

'Er, hello?' called Amy.

'QUAAAARRRRRK! QUAAAARRRRRK!' replied the bird.

'Do you think it's a seagull or a duck?' Boo asked.

'I'm not sure,' said Ruth, 'it sounds like a cross between the two.'

'Whatever it is, it doesn't seem very interested in us,' Amy complained. There was still no sign of the bird, although from the sound of it, it must be close. She flew closer to the rock face and landed on a narrow ledge. 'Hey, birdy!' she called. 'We know you're there somewhere. Stop hiding. We need to talk to you.'

At that moment an enormous duck-shaped bill poked out of a crack at the end of the ledge. It opened to reveal row upon row of razor-sharp teeth.

Amy stared at it. Was it one of the granny raptors? *Surely not!* They couldn't fly. She watched in fascinated horror as the creature squeezed itself out of its hiding place. After the bill came a green head and neck, a brown chest, and a plump buff-coloured body supported on a pair of bright orange webbed feet. Unlike the granny raptors the creature was fully feathered. Around its neck was a bow tie.

Amy regarded it in astonishment. *James Pond!* He wasn't dead after all! Raptorov had used him for one of his evil dino-bird experiments.

'Barn it!' shouted Ruth. 'He's turned Pond into a ptero-duck-tyl!'

'QUAAAARRRRRK! QUAAAARRRRRK! SSSSSSSSSSSSSSSSSSS!'

The ptero-duck-tyl bared its teeth and let out an

angry hiss. It began to unfurl its long, bony wings.

'Amy, get away from the ledge!' Boo cried.

Amy didn't need telling twice. She took off with a terrified squawk.

James Pond positioned himself on the edge of the ledge and extended his wings to full stretch. Before – when he was a normal mallard duck – his wingspan had been less than a metre. Now that he was a ptero-duck-tyl, it was more than two. Nor did he need a run-up in order to take off any more. With one flap of his wings he was airborne. He shot after Amy.

'Helllllllllpppppppp!' screamed Amy.

'Put the flight booster to ROCKET BLAST MAX!' Boo shouted.

Amy twiddled the controls. She felt a surge of power as the ROCKET BLAST mode kicked in. Even so, the ptero-duck-tyl was gaining on her.

'Take evasive action!' Ruth yelled.

Amy flew this way and that, trying to shake off the dino-duck, but James Pond stuck tenaciously to her tail. *SNAP! SNAP! SNAP!* His jaws opened and closed like a great white shark's.

The flight booster engine began to splutter. 'It's no good,' she squawked. 'I'm losing power. Mayday, mayday!'

'Leave it to me,' Boo shouted. 'You two, get to safety. This could get messy.' She gave a whistle. 'Hey, duck-face! Over here!'

The ptero-duck-tyl looked round. Hovering a few metres away from him was a plump, honey-coloured chicken with feathery boots. It looked ripe for the kill. It wasn't even trying to get away, unlike the small brown one with the puffy tummy. The dino-duck was hungry. It couldn't remember when it had last eaten. Only that it had been stuck up on a ledge for hours on end waiting for its tea.

WHOOSH! The ptero-duck-tyl circled away from Amy and closed in on Boo.

Boo waited until the last possible second, then she set her flight booster to ROCKET BLAST EXTRA MAX and whizzed upwards out of the dino-duck's flight path. The ptero-duck-tyl circled for a second time. Again Boo waited. Then once she was sure it had her in its sights she zoomed off.

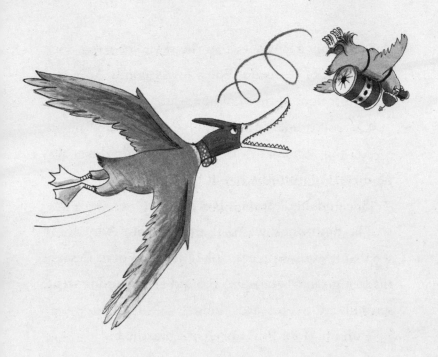

Ruth and Amy had taken shelter in a tiny crevice. They peeped out. There was nothing they could do now. It was up to Boo. All they could hope was that she was as good at flying as she was at gymnastics.

Boo zigzagged this way and that in an amazing display of aerobatics, the ptero-duck-tyl close behind. She did two loop-the-loops and then she began to climb. Up and up she went. Up and up and up, until

she was only a tiny speck in the sky. The dino-duck followed like a missile. For a few seconds Amy and Ruth lost sight of them. They waited anxiously.

'Do you think she's okay?' Amy whispered.

At that moment Boo reappeared. She was plummeting from the sky at breath-taking speed.

'She's cut her engine!' Ruth gasped.

The dino-duck was still after her but Amy could see that it was losing control. The speed of its descent made it go into a tailspin. Round and round it went, spiralling down towards the sea.

'Pull up, Boo! Pull up!' Ruth breathed.

Amy was too scared to say anything. It looked for the world as if Boo and the ptero-duck-tyl would both crash.

VROOM! At the very last minute Boo turned the engine of the flight booster back on. She put her wings above her head in an elegant pose and swept upwards in a beautiful arc, like a circus performer on a trapeze.

The ptero-duck-tyl tried desperately to pull out of its spin, but it was too late. The dino-duck

crashed straight into the sea with a loud splash and disappeared.

'Oh dear,' said Boo, landing beside the others. 'I think I've just killed James Pond.'

The three chickens flew low over the sea, looking anxiously for signs of the dino-duck.

'Wait – what's that?' Ruth said, pointing to an object floating nearby.

'It's him! It's James Pond!' Amy said.

The dip in the ocean seemed to have done the duck agent some good. The ptero-duck-tyl had turned back into an ordinary mallard once more.

'Where am I?' he said groggily, paddling in circles, a confused expression on his face.

The three chickens glanced at one another. There was no way James Pond was fit for the mission. They would have to come back for him later. Together they guided the stricken duck agent to the shore, found a sheltered spot and made him a bed from dried seaweed. James Pond staggered onto his makeshift bed and fell asleep at once.

The three chickens fitted the walkie-thinkies into

their ears so that Raptorov couldn't tune in to their conversation.

'I knew something like this would happen,' Amy said crossly in her head.

The others nodded. The walkie-thinkies worked perfectly!

'Actually it's a good thing James Pond was turned into a ptero-duck-tyl,' Ruth remarked back.

'Why?' asked Amy in surprise. Ruth hadn't sounded this cheerful in ages. It was as if she'd just solved a SUPER DIFFICULT Sudoku puzzle.

'Because it's shown us that Raptorov's experiments aren't permanent. It's like Boo hoped: the dinosaur DNA wears off! It's probably because it's so old. With any luck the granny raptors will soon turn back to normal too.'

'So what's the plan?' Amy said.

The walkie-thinkie went quiet while Ruth thought for a minute. 'The main thing is to get rid of Raptorov,' she said. 'I think James Pond was right for once. If Thaddeus sees that we've defeated his new best buddy, he's not going to hang around and risk getting his whiskers full of mites again. Then we can destroy the laboratory, rescue the flock and get out of there.'

'I'll fit the homing device,' Amy offered bravely. 'Ruth, you're the scientist. You should deal with the laboratory.'

'Which leaves *me* creating a distraction.' Boo's voice came over the walkie-thinkie for the first time. She grinned. 'I've had an idea about that, by the way. But we might want to get a move on, before the granny hens' raptor juice wears off.' She told the others her idea.

'That's brilliant!' Amy chortled.

'I can't wait to see Raptorov's face!' Ruth agreed.

'So, what are we waiting for?' Boo said, taking the owl cave sat-nav out of the Emergency Chicken Pack. 'Let's do it!'

Inside his bed cave Thaddeus was getting ready for the feast. The granny raptors were safely locked away in their prison quarters and the chickens from Stormy

Cliff Caravan Park were chilling in the larder. He hadn't actually killed any of them yet: he liked his chicken fresh. Best of all, Professor Rooster's elite-chicken squad would have been eaten by the ptero-duck-tyl by now. Life was good!

He admired his reflection in the mirror. Looking back at him, elegant in top hat, tails and a silk waistcoat was the dandiest, sassiest, most handsome fox that he had ever seen. *Him!* Yes, he could still do with putting on a couple more kilos, but the feast to come would soon fix that. Then he would be fully restored to the Thaddeus E. Fox of old. With the army of granny raptors at his side and no elite-chicken squad to spoil his plans, nothing could stop him. He picked up his cane and gave it a twirl. Then he pattered off down the tunnel towards the laboratory to find his new friend.

As he expected, Raptorov was hard at work on his experiments, listening to *Swan Lake*.

Daaaaa – du-du-du-du-du – da-daaaa – da-daaaa – du-du-du-du-du – daaaaa.

The music crashed and boomed.

'Thaddeus!' the owl hooted, catching sight of him. 'Your timing is perfect. We both have something to celebrate!'

'We do?' said Thaddeus noncommittally. He didn't want to bring on another big-head evil baddie speech by asking too many questions.

The owl's eyes twinkled. 'Guess what I found on the beach tonight while your granny raptors were at work stocking the larder?'

'A fossil?' Thaddeus hazarded.

'Yes, a fossil!' Raptorov clicked his beak impatiently. 'But not just any fossil. The fossil of a T. rex claw!'

'Cool,' said Thaddeus. 'What are you going to do with it?'

'Do? Twit twoo! I have already extracted the DNA.' Raptorov waved a test tube at the fox. Now all I need is to find the right bird to try it out on. It's my next step towards world domination. We must celebrate together.'

'Shall I start the fire for the feast?' Thaddeus said hopefully. He felt famished.

'Just let me tidy up here a bit first,' Raptorov said.

 152

He labelled the T. rex DNA and placed the test tube carefully in a rack, then he shuffled about, collecting his equipment.

'Er, do you think we could listen to something a bit more cheerful while you do that?' Thaddeus asked politely. He found *Swan Lake* a bit gloomy.

'Of course! I know just the thing!' Raptorov chuckled. He shuffled over to an old CD player.

The delicate sound of orchestral violins being plucked dinked around the laboratory cave. Very soon a glockenspiel took up the melody.

Da-da-da-da — da-da — duh-duh-duh — duh-duh-duh — duh-duh-duh — do-de-do-de-do!

Thaddeus found his foot tapping in time to the music. It was a jaunty little tune — probably his favourite Tchaikovsky so far. 'What's that one called?' he asked.

'It's the "Dance of the Sugar Plum Fairy", from the ballet, *The Nutcracker,*' Raptorov replied.

Dunalalalaa — do-de-do-do — di-di — duh-duh-duh — duh-duh-duh — duh-duh-duh — da-di-da-di-da!

'Excellent!' Thaddeus laughed. He felt like dancing

himself, although ballet wasn't his thing: he preferred the foxtrot.

But someone else *did* prefer ballet. For just at that moment a beautiful honey-coloured hen wearing a purple ballet outfit pirouetted into the laboratory and began to perform a perfect *pas de deux*.

Thaddeus's eyes bulged. He'd know that chicken anywhere! It was the sporty one who did gymnastics from Professor Rooster's elite-chicken squad. He felt his self-confidence drain away. Raptorov had *promised* him the ptero-duck-tyl would kill all three of them before they even made it to Stormy Island, yet at least one of them had survived. And here she was, prancing about the laboratory as if she didn't give a flying feather that it contained two evil villains who would devour her on sight. He fought back tears of frustration. That was the problem with Professor Rooster and his team: they didn't understand BOUNDARIES! And if the sporty one had survived, then the others probably had too. They'd be out there somewhere in the caves plotting to commit some nastiness upon his person. Even the thought of his army of granny raptors no

longer filled him with confidence. If Professor Rooster's squad could survive a ptero-duck-tyl attack, who was to say that they wouldn't defeat the grannies? He had to warn Raptorov.

'Ch-ch-ch-ch-chicken!' he stuttered, pointing his cane shakily at Boo. 'Pro-pro-pro-pro Roo-roo-roo-roo-rooster!'

Raptorov didn't respond immediately. His unblinking eyes were fixed on Boo.

Da-da-da-da — da-da — duh-duh-duh — duh-duh-duh — duh-duh-duh — do-de-do-de-do!

Dunalalalaa — do-de-do-do — di-di — duh-duh-duh — duh-duh-duh — duh-duh-duh — da-di-da-di-da!

'Fascinating!' Raptorov seemed entranced by the spectacle. 'To survive the ptero-duck-tyl and then give a performance such as this! Just think, Thaddeus, what I could do with the DNA of this hen.'

'What?' squealed Thaddeus, aghast. The idea of more birds in the world with Boo's DNA was horrific. 'Why don't you just eat it?'

'Because if I extract its DNA first, I could create a whole ballet troop to entertain me!' Raptorov replied. His eyes had taken on a dreamy look. 'Not hens, of course, but something more elegant: flamingos, for example.'

Flamingos? Thaddeus felt panic rise. He'd been so excited about the prospect of revenge he'd lost sight of how mad Raptorov really was.

At that moment the music came to an end.

'More!' hooted Raptorov in delight. 'Bravo!'

Boo gave a deep curtsy. 'Give me a minute.' She

156

pirouetted over to the CD player, slipped a disc from under her ballet outfit and put it on in place of *The Nutcracker*.

Thaddeus E. Fox watched with growing concern. 'I don't think this is a good idea, Vladimir,' he said nervously. Boo's actions had all the hallmarks of a classic chicken-squad sting. Thaddeus knew their methods by now. One of them distracted you while the other two got ready to do something unmentionable. And it was happening again, right under their noses. He just knew it.

'Nonsense, my friend!' the owl chuckled. 'What can one small hen do against the great Vladimir Alexei Raptorov?'

Boo gave the owl an innocent smile. Then she turned the volume to FULL BLAST and pressed PLAY.

Chapter Sixteen

BOOM-BOOM-NA-NA-NA
BOOM-BOOM-NA-NA-NA

The laboratory resonated with a deafeningly loud disco beat. It bounced off the floor and walls until they shook. A few loose test tubes fell onto the floor and smashed.

'AAAAAAARRRRRRGGGGHHHHH!' Raptorov screeched. He wrapped his wings over his ears. The disco music was playing havoc with his supersonic hearing. It felt as if someone were playing the drums in his head. 'HVREK! HVREK! HVREK!' he screeched. 'Stop that horrible racket!'

'It's not a horrible racket. It's called "The Funky Chicken",' Boo shouted back. 'And it's a lot more fun than boring old Tchaikovsky.'

'How dare you!' Vladimir roared. 'Tchaikovsky is the greatest composer that ever lived.' He hunched himself into the owl threat pose and made a grab for

Boo with his enormous wings.

'Down low, too slow!' Boo taunted, somersaulting out of his reach.

Raptorov tried again. But Boo was too quick for him. This time she did a backflip.

'Catch her, Thaddeus!' shouted Raptorov. 'But remember, I want this hen alive!'

'I can't!' Thaddeus E. Fox cowered in the corner.

'Thaddeus,' Raptorov rasped, 'get a grip on yourself. It is just a dancing chicken. There is nothing to be scared of.'

Reluctantly, Thaddeus got to his feet.

Boo tumbled towards the entrance of the laboratory and disappeared.

Just then they heard a commotion in the tunnel outside.

'SQUAWWWKKKKKKKK-KA-KA-KA-KA!'

It was the granny raptors.

'I thought I told you to lock the cage?' Raptorov rounded on Thaddeus.

'I did!' Thaddeus protested. 'I left the key on the hook, just like you said.'

The commotion was getting louder. The granny raptors were approaching the laboratory.

'THIS WAY TO THE DISCO!' cried a voice from the tunnel. 'Come along, everyone!'

Thaddeus's whiskers trembled. The voice belonged to the smallest of Professor Rooster's chicken warriors. The one with the fluffy tummy and the wrestling moves.

'SQUAWWWKKKKKKKK-KA-KA-KA-KA!'

'Here we are!' said the voice. 'In you go. After the food.'

'What food?' Raptorov hooted. 'There is no food.'

Just then a small chicken clad in a suit of full body armour stepped into the laboratory. It was carrying a mite blaster.

 160

'Hello, Thaddeus,' said Amy from underneath the helmet. 'Remember me?'

No no no no no! 'Get out of the way!' Thaddeus shouted to the owl. 'It's full of mites!'

'Actually it's full of genetically modified worms,' Amy corrected him. 'Ruth swapped them over.' She pulled the trigger.

The two villains were engulfed.

Thaddeus screamed. The worms were in his whiskers. They were in his fur. They were down his neck and under his hat. One of them was even trying to eat his eyeballs.

Raptorov was covered too. He danced from foot to foot, shaking his feathers.

Amy gave a whistle. 'Supper time!' she shouted.

Thaddeus peered through the fog of worms. To his horror the laboratory was filling up with granny raptors on zimmer frames, all grooving to the beat of 'The Funky Chicken'. The meanest, ugliest one sniffed the air. Her eyes lit up.

'WOOORRRMMMMMS!' she shrilled.

The villains found themselves engulfed for a second time. This time by granny raptors, pecking for food.

'Do something, Raptorov!' Thaddeus begged as a huge set of false raptor teeth came perilously close to chewing his whiskers.

The eagle owl hunched over and spread his wings wide. 'HVRECK! HVRECK! HVRECK!' he screeched, shuffling forward.

The granny raptors punched the air with their zimmer frames in delight.

'SQUAWWWKKKKKKKK-KA-KA-KA-KA!' they screeched back.

'Not that, you stupid owl!' Thaddeus shouted.
'They think it's a dance move! Do something else!'

Back at the entrance of the laboratory, Ruth was
preparing the homing device. The first part of Boo's
plan had worked perfectly, now it was time for the
second part.

'All you have to do is clip the homing device to
Raptorov's leg while he's not looking,' Ruth told
Amy through the walkie-thinkie. 'I've set the co-
ordinates. Once it's fixed in place you push the

button and the missile technology will take him straight back to Russia. If you have any trouble with Thaddeus we'll cover you with the mite blaster.'

'Okay,' said Amy, taking the pliers awkwardly in one wing and the homing device in the other. It was hard to hold onto them when you were wearing a suit of full body armour.

'Watch out for Raptorov's talons,' Boo reminded her. 'Good luck!'

Amy advanced into the laboratory. She made her way round the edge of the cave towards the villains. The plan was to creep up on Raptorov from behind and fix the homing device to his leg before he realised what was happening. He was already disorientated by the loud disco music. Now all his attention was fixed on fighting off the frenzied granny raptors.

The plan would work as long as Granny Wishbone and her cronies kept dancing and pecking.

Amy bumped along under the workbench, keeping as close to the wall as she could. Through the throng of wrinkly granny raptors, she could see the owl's long feathered legs next to a pair of red-

coated trembling ones that belonged to Thaddeus. She pushed her way forwards into the melee, wings outstretched.

Just then something happened. One by one the grannies stopped dancing. They lay on their backs with their legs in the air, snoring. Amy watched in horror. Their beaks were shrinking. And their raptor claws were turning back into chicken toes. The raptor DNA was wearing off! She had to act now or it would be too late.

Amy darted forward. She looped the homing device around Raptorov's leg and tightened it with the pliers. She reached for the button.

But Raptorov had come to his senses. He lashed out with his other leg and kicked her away.

Amy flew through the air. She landed painfully in a heap on Raptorov's workbench. She sat up, dazed.

There was silence in the cave. The CD had finished.

'HVRECK! HVRECK! HVRECK!' The angry owl advanced on Amy. 'You think you can destroy me?' he said. 'Well you are wrong. My dino-birds

165

will still rule the world. But you and your friends, you are finished.'

'What do you mean, rule the world?' Amy said. This was bigger than any of them – even Ruth – had thought.

Raptorov let out a screech of laughter. 'You thought this was it? Then more fool you – twit twoo. This is just the beginning. In time I shall create a super-species of dino-birds who will rule over the world like they did millions of years ago, with me as their leader.' He blinked. 'But first I shall tear you all to shreds for daring to challenge the greatest bird that ever lived.'

'We're not scared of you!' Boo and Ruth flew over to the workbench and stood either side of Amy. Boo raised the mite blaster and fired.

'A few mites aren't going to stop the great Vladimir Alexei Raptorov!' the owl hooted. He reached out his wing and tossed the mite blaster aside with a flick of his feathers. The gadget spun across the floor. 'Now which one of you shall I devour first?'

Amy looked around desperately for something

to save them. They were out of weapons. Her little chicken brain thought frantically. Maybe she could throw a fossil at Raptorov and stun him while the others went for the button on the homing device? But there were no fossils on the part of the workbench where she had landed. Only a rack of test tubes. One of the labels caught her eye.

T. REX DNA – HIGHLY DANGEROUS

She blinked. *T. rex DNA?* Ruth had said chickens were related to the T. rex, which meant it couldn't do that much harm. And it might be their only chance to escape. 'Don't worry,' she told her friends. 'I've got it covered.' Before anyone could stop her she jumped to her feet, scuttled over to the test tube and downed the contents.

'NOOOOOOOOOOOOO!' screeched Raptorov.

Amy felt herself growing. Huge claws sprouted from her feet. Her legs felt strong and powerful. She even had a tail! Her head crashed against the ceiling of the cave. She was definitely more of a dinosaur

than a bird, she decided. It must be in her blood, like Ruth said.

She jumped off the workbench. Raptorov was tiny! He cowered beneath her, quivering with fear. Out of one eye she caught a glimpse of Thaddeus racing out of the laboratory, his tail between his legs.

Amy let out a great roar.

'RRRROOOOOAAAAAAARRRRRRR.'

The owl covered his face with his wings.

'Go, Boo, go!' Ruth shouted through the walkie-thinkie. 'Push the button.'

Boo dropped down off the workbench. She ran between Amy's huge feet to where Raptorov was standing and pushed the button on the homing device. The owl was lifted into the air.

'HVRECK! HVRECK! HVRECK! HVRECK!' Raptorov flapped his wings frantically but try as he might he couldn't overcome the homing device. His cries faded as he shot out of the laboratory, back through the system of tunnels and away from Stormy Island in the direction of Russia.

Amy let out a delighted giggle. The flock was safe.

And she was surprised to find that she was already back to her original size. Luckily, the T. rex DNA had worn off quickly. It had been fun being a T. rex for a short time, she thought, but she was glad she wasn't stuck like that forever. She liked being a chicken, especially a chicken warrior. Ev-o-lu-shun wasn't such a bad thing after all, although she wished she'd grown a bigger brain, like Ruth.

The three chickens removed the walkie-thinkies from their ears. They threw themselves on their backs next to the grannies, their legs in the air.

'Phew!' said Ruth, 'that was close!'

'Very,' agreed Boo, 'I thought for a minute we might not make it.'

'It was kind of fun, though, you've got to admit,' said Amy. She felt sure that Professor Rooster would be proud of them (although he might not be happy that she'd turned into a dinosaur!). She let out a contented sigh. 'Chicken mission accomplished,' she said.

Epilogue

Two days later . . .

The park keeper drove along the coast road towards Stormy Cliff Caravan Park. She was in a good mood. It was Sunday; she'd had a lie-in and read the morning paper. Now she just had time to check on the chicken flock before lunch. She'd been invited for roast beef with her daughter and the grandkids down at their house in the town and she didn't want to be late.

She passed the derelict farmhouse. A fox was walking along the wall. It seemed to be having trouble balancing. Then the park keeper realised – the poor thing didn't have a tail! There were quite a lot of foxes around these parts, she'd noticed, especially at the farmhouse. And all of them seemed to either be a bit crock or a bit timid. Not at all like the ones in town that her daughter was always complaining about. They were as bold as brass. She smiled to herself. Perhaps the foxes at the farm were there to get away from it all. Perhaps they liked the peace and quiet of Stormy Cliff. She chuckled. Perhaps it was a sort of foxy convalescent home for distressed foxes! *Ha-ha-ha!*

She switched on the radio.

'In breaking news, scientists in Russia report that Vladimir the Eagle Owl has returned to their laboratory,' the newscaster said. 'The genetically modified owl went missing several weeks ago and was thought to have disappeared for good. However, he apparently found his way back to the laboratory with the help of a sophisticated homing device strapped to his leg. Scientists have appealed for more information . . .

Extraordinary! thought the park keeper. *A genetically modified owl! And how on earth did he end up with a homing device strapped to his leg?*

'And in another amazing bird story, scientists have discovered that chickens share the same DNA as the T. rex . . .'

Amazing! Thought the park keeper. *Chickens related to a T. rex?* You couldn't make it up!

She pulled up at the caravan park and got out of the van.

Everything looked just as normal. The flock was grazing peacefully in the field, the caravans were empty and there wasn't a soul to be seen. It always amazed her that the place was so empty, apart from the occasional fossil hunter of course. The caves on Stormy Island were supposed to be the best place to find fossils (although personally she'd never been, as the island reminded her too much of a giant tombstone!). She took a lungful of fresh air, trying to imagine what Stormy Cliff had looked like in the Jurassic age. Then, mindful of the time, she strode towards the caravan where the chickens slept at night to replenish their food.

It was then that she noticed that the door was hanging open on another of the caravans – the one nearest to the loos. She frowned. It looked like someone had broken in!

She pushed open the door of the caravan and went

inside. The place was a tip! There were feathers and bits of food scattered everywhere. *Chickens!* But it wasn't like her girls to break into another caravan. Or to leave such a revolting mess. The flock had their own caravan, and they were usually very tidy. It really was most odd!

She took a step forward. *CRUNCH!* The park keeper bent down and picked up a piece of squashed metal. She scratched her head, trying to work out what it was. It had three legs and a bar at the top, almost like a chicken-sized zimmer frame, although of course it couldn't be that, unless a bunch of old granny chickens had taken it into their heads to come and stay in her caravan while she wasn't there! It was probably just an old water bottle holder off a bike.

Even so . . .

The park keeper's eyes twinkled.

A seaside home for convalescent foxes . . .

A genetically modified eagle owl . . .

A dinosaur chicken . . .

A bunch of granny hens . . .

All you needed was a decent setting (*Stormy Cliff?*)

and a few superheroes (*an elite-chicken squad and their mentor perhaps?*) and you had the makings of a good story! Now what could she call it? How about *The Mystery of Stormy Island*? Her granddaughter would love that. Perhaps she could make something up to tell her at bedtime?

The park keeper finished her chores quickly and got back into the van. The more she thought about it, the more excited she felt. The story was really taking shape in her head. She already had her first line. It went something like this:

Far to the north, on a remote clifftop stands Stormy Cliff Caravan Park . . .

Find out about
other crimes the
Elite Chicken Squad
have foxed . . .

If you love

Chicken Mission

Then you'll love Atticus Claw,
the world's greatest
cat burglar!

Read on for a sneak peek of
his first adventure:

ATTICUS CLAW
Breaks the Law

Atticus Grammaticus Cattypuss Claw – the world's greatest cat burglar – was lying on a comfy bed in Monte Carlo when a messenger pigeon landed on the window ledge. Atticus opened one eye, then the other. Finally, with a yawn, he stretched lazily, jumped off the bed and padded over towards the window.

'Are you Claw?' The messenger pigeon said cautiously.

'Who's asking?' Atticus replied, examining his sharp talons.

'Never you mind.' The pigeon shivered. He blinked at Atticus. He had been told to deliver the note to a brown-and-black-striped tabby with a chewed ear, four white socks and a red handkerchief with its name embroidered on it tied round its neck. He was sure he'd got the right cat. It looked a nasty piece of work; but then most cats did as far as he was concerned. 'I've got a message for you.'

'Hand it over then,' Atticus purred, jumping on to a table and holding out a paw.

'No chance!' the pigeon sidled away from him along the ledge. Carefully, watching Atticus all the time with his beady eyes, he unclipped the tube containing the message from his leg and threw it on the table.

Atticus flipped off the lid, reached in with a claw and uncurled a tiny piece of paper. He stared at the message. It was in a strange scratchy writing he didn't recognise.

To: Atticus Grammaticus
    Cattypuss Claw

We have a job for you. Meet
us on Tuesday. Littleton-on-Sea.
11.15. At the pier. Don't be
late.

Come alone. Or else.

PS: It will be worth your while.

'Who gave you this?' Atticus demanded.

The pigeon looked frightened. 'I can't remember,' he cooed.

Suddenly Atticus pounced. His left paw pinned the pigeon's tail. 'Don't waste my time,' he hissed. 'I want to know who gave you this.'

The pigeon looked more frightened than ever. 'I can't say,' he squawked. 'They'll kill me if I do. And worse! You're not supposed to find out until you get there. Help! I'm in a tizzy!' The pigeon fainted.

Atticus let go. 'Hmmm,' he said, reading the message again. 'Interesting . . .' He glanced at the dazed bird. Pigeons always talked. Yet this one had kept its beak shut. Whoever had sent the message, Atticus decided, had certainly scared the poo out of the pigeon.

For a moment he hesitated, wondering what to do. Then he grinned. All cats like mysteries – that's why they're called 'curious'. And Atticus was no exception. In fact Atticus *loved* a mystery. Especially when he was at the centre of it.

The pigeon came to with a start. 'Well?' he trembled. 'What shall I tell them?'

'I'll be there,' Atticus said.

The pigeon looked relieved.

'Off you go, then.' With a sweep of his paw, Atticus pushed the startled bird off the ledge.

He watched it flap away. Then he padded down the stairs and went into the study. The computer was on. He tapped out the words *Littleton-on-Sea* expertly with his claws. A picture of a sleepy cobbled town next to a flat grey sea popped up on the screen. It didn't look much, Atticus thought. Not exactly the sort of place you'd expect a summer crime wave. But he could soon change that! Tapping away at the keyboard, it didn't take him long to work out exactly how he was going to get there. Then, without a backward glance, he slipped out of the cat flap, jumped on a train to the nearest port and boarded the next cruise ship to England.

JENNIFER GRAY

ATTICUS CLAW

CLAW

Breaks the Law

'Atticus puts the
WOW! into meow!'
Jeremy Strong

ff

Out Now!

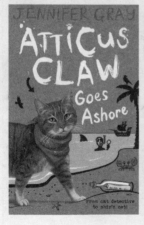

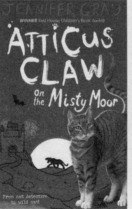